D1609057

the
ALICE FAYE
MOVIE BOOK

the ALICE FAYE MOVIE BOOK

W. FRANKLYN MOSHIER

A & W VISUAL LIBRARY

For the A.F.C.C.
with grateful thanks
one and all

Alice Faye

Acknowledgments

**For their help in the preparation of this book,
the author wishes to thank the following for their advice,
interest, and sincere cooperation.**

*Locating and loan of articles and reviews
dealing directly with Alice Faye and her films:*

The Academy of Motion Picture Arts and Sciences,
Earl Anderson, John Cocchi, Richard Mayfield,
William Ramsay, Jack Tillmany and to Arthur Nicholson
for providing reviews of Faye films of the various
English publications mentioned herein and his views
on "Fair Faye—The English Favorite."

*Loan of portraits and stills to augment the author's
personal collection:*

Roy Bishop, Robert Board, Alice Faye, William Faye,
Alex Goldberg, Peter Oos and Robert Epstein.

Loan of sheet music:

Philip Haggard, Robert Grimes and Robert Johnson.
A special thank you to Mr. Grimes, not only for use of
his collection of sheet music, but who tirelessly provided
song titles, names of composers, and carefully proofread
the galleys for musical discrepancies.

Assistance in identification of supporting players:

Mr. Chuck Lindsley

Proofreading:

Gerald Wyckoff and William Berner

Layout and graphics:

Chuck Thayer—CTA Graphics—San Francisco

Typesetting:

Richard W. Brown Composition Service—San Francisco

*A very special note of thanks to Mr. Alex Gordon
of 20th Century-Fox Film Corporation for arranging
special screenings of the first four Faye films plus
innumerable suggestions and encouragement.*

Table of Contents

One of the most honored and respected men in his profession, Henry King directed fifty films in a quarter century association with 20th Century-Fox.
Three of these starred Alice Faye and rank among her finest screen appearances.

FOREWORD
by Mr. Henry King

It is an honor for me to provide a foreword to this very attractive book, for the name Alice Faye evokes some wonderfully happy memories in a time which seems just like yesterday. Times have changed and movies have changed, but I hope that Alice Faye has not. Not only is she my favorite actress, she is also a favorite person.

My association with Alice Faye began in 1937 when I was given a film to direct which later became IN OLD CHICAGO. At that time it had the working title of MRS. O'LEARY'S COW, which was fortunately changed after we went into actual production. Mr. Zanuck, Vice President in charge of production at Twentieth Century-Fox, insisted that the two lead roles should be played by Clark Gable and Jean Harlow, and while I greatly admired Clark's work, I felt he was too old to be believable as Alice Brady's son. Audiences would never forgive him at the end, but they would forgive a headstrong younger man. Jean's tragic death that summer almost ended in an indefinite postponement of the picture.

I never worked on a motion picture that I didn't believe in, and I thoroughly and completely believed in that script. It wasn't difficult to convince the powers that be that a young man named *Power* would be ideal for the role of Dion. But casting the pivotal role of Belle was quite another matter. It had to be someone with fire, not just a pretty face; it had to be someone capable of conveying depth of characterization; and it had to be someone who could sing the three numbers with style. I could see only one person for the part, and I went right to the top and asked for Alice Faye.

Up to that time Alice had appeared in a series of highly popular and profitable musical pictures which spotlighted her natural singing voice but made little if any demands upon her acting ability. I made a very short test of her in which she was seated at her dressing table. Spying Power in the mirror she was to register anger, turn and hurl a jar of cold cream at him. The emotion and few words she uttered came right from the guts. You've got to be an actress to do that.

But the real "test" came shortly thereafter when we filmed the carriage sequence in which Ty kidnapped Belle. There were just the two of them in a rather long scene which ran to about three pages calling for acting ability and acting alone. We rehearsed it a couple of times and then shot it without a cut or a break. It was perfect. When that sequence was run the following day my faith in Alice Faye as an actress was vindicated. Mr. Zanuck called in every available producer, director, and technician he could find. He announced that we had a new "actress" at Twentieth Century-Fox. Alice Faye was on her way.

Alice Faye is a very sensitive person—she's Irish—she could fight one moment and cry the next. She had lots of spirit to be sure, but I realized right from the start that she seemed unsure of her own ability. I knew I could inspire confidence in her and bring out that sense of natural accomplishment so important to a really fine actress. I work differently from many directors, but I have never found it necessary to raise my voice or shout at my cast or crew. It pays off in the long run when you are involved in this very complicated and exacting business of making motion pictures. I knew that Alice would deliver a first-rate performance as Belle, but she had to feel I was on her side, capable of sympathetic understanding while at the same time explaining carefully just what I wanted.

We clicked — Alice and I. She, like most sensitive, talented people, needed to feel she was doing it herself, not just aping a director's instructions. She always took direction beautifully without any show of temperament, and when you were done the character she played came across with a vibrant warmth of personality so many actresses did not possess. I think that was the secret of Alice's success in pictures. A deep-seated human warmth, so genuine, so real that everyone felt it. It's truly a gift; you can't buy it. It's either there or it isn't.

Alice was a grand comedienne, she had tremendous emotion, but she was not a studied actress—not that Actor's Studio type which became popular later on. She was a natural performer with a natural talent and a singing voice capable of selling a song like nobody else. In later years I did not always feel she got the material which she could do best.

There was a magic about Alice Faye which I found thoroughly refreshing and vastly stimulating. I used her again as Stella in ALEXANDER'S RAGTIME BAND, and again Ty Power and Don Ameche starred with her. I called them my "Happy Trio," because there was a wonderful chemistry when those three gifted young people worked together. For years I've had their photographs together on my wall.

Alice and I worked together one more time in LITTLE OLD NEW YORK, which proved that the Faye singing voice didn't need to be employed to result in an outstanding performance. She had an inborn talent and feel for comedy. That was a wonderfully relaxed and happy company and a fine slice of Americana.

I've been extremely fortunate in a long career of directing. I don't claim to be a starmaker by any means, though the term has been applied now and again. I do think though in retrospect that the good Lord put me in a position to help a number of people realize their potential in this business of making motion pictures. I like to think that the great transition in Alice's acting life from singer to dramatic actress took place with me. In a number of cases I've helped to change the careers and maybe the lives of some wonderfully gifted people.

I'm glad one of them was Alice Faye.

Henry King
North Hollywood, Calif.

Introduction

THE ALICE FAYE MOVIE BOOK is a labor of love, presented as a tribute to one of the screen's greatest musical stars. It is the culmination of years of genuine adoration and appreciation of a personality, which it seems to me, is second to none.

I discovered Alice Faye at a very tender age when she played Belle Fawcett in IN OLD CHICAGO. At the time I was swept into a morass of emotion for the "beautiful lady" and worked myself into a state of near collapse as only a child can. I was sure that Tyrone Power had broken her heart (the cad), and worst of all I *knew* that fire would spare every no-account and gleefully consume Miss Belle, and I should never see her again. But the movies didn't often end that way in the halcyon days of 1938, and Miss Faye survived only to be hurt again by other leading men.

The years passed, the boy grew up, but the films continued to work their magic in countless hours of viewing until I knew every gesture, every vocal inflection she exhibited on the screen.

In the pages that follow I have tried to be perfectly objective about the screen work of Alice Faye. Though my adoration has dimmed not one bit, I have attempted to document in my notes and quoted film reviews that *all* Faye films were not the screen masterpieces of say an ALEXANDER'S RAGTIME BAND. If Miss Faye does not come across on the screen for all people as a "great actress" it must be admitted that for the type of roles she essayed in her career she was indeed a "very capable actress" with a surprising depth and range. One has only to compare her performance in a trifle like SHE LEARNED ABOUT SAILORS with the controlled adroitness of her Molly Adair in HOLLYWOOD CAVALCADE, to see the degree of professional brilliance of which she was capable.

To illustrate Alice Faye's standing in the field of popular music, I have included a sampling of at least one published song from each of her films, if a number was used at any time in the production. Her picture on the cover of sheet music sold more copies than that of any picture star of her time, and dedicated collectors today know the value of many of these song sheets from the past.

For the nit-picking movie purist hunting for mistakes in the many names which are to be found herein, let me say that these names were taken directly from the credits of the films themselves and not from some reference source. If they are in disagreement with a previously published work, then one can only assume that they were flashed upon the movie screens of the world in that fashion.

This book then is offered as a record of the screen work of one of the loveliest ladies ever to step foot on a studio sound stage. It is my hope that it will inspire others to undertake similar tasks of their favorites so that the musical film will take its rightful place in the history of motion pictures.

W. Franklyn Moshier

San Francisco, California
July 31, 1971

THE
FABULOUS
FAYE

Dressed in a deep blue evening gown decorated with reflecting sequins, she leaned languidly against a terrace pillar and in a deep throaty voice sang "Tropical Magic." The year was 1941, the picture WEEK-END IN HAVANA, and the blue-eyed blonde was Alice Faye, known to millions of movie goers the world over as the screen's foremost exponent of popular song.

WEEK-END IN HAVANA was her twenty-eighth film since her debut in 1934 in GEORGE WHITE'S SCANDALS. For eleven years as a top star at 20th Century-Fox she was starred with the greatest names in the business: Spencer Tracy, Dick Powell, Robert Young, John Payne, Jack Oakie, and her perennial costar, Don Ameche. Three times she costarred with Tyrone Power, the greatest male box-office draw of the late thirties and forties. Like Power, Alice Faye's screen potential was so great that only twice in her career was she loaned to competing studios. In early 1940, proof of her industry-wide standing came when the *Showmen's Trade Review* on January thirteenth named her the nation's outstanding female box-office Star, ranking above Myrna Loy and Bette Davis and just behind Mickey Rooney and Tyrone Power.

Composers eagerly sought to have their songs introduced by Alice, and one such distinguished tunesmith, none other than Irving Berlin, openly admitted, "I'd rather have Alice Faye introduce my songs than anyone else."

Faye was not a typical star personality of her day. While she worked hard, gave vent to no outbursts of temperament, was well-liked by all her coworkers, she admitted that she was not overly ambitious and professed to being a lazy sort of person. This "lazy person" often turned up in four starring roles per year. She was a leading star for nearly twelve years in a time when seven was considered a long life at the top, and she retired of her own volition when her worth as a star was at its zenith. Her screen roles were always star parts; she never played bits or worked as an extra. In her first thirty-two films she was never billed lower than third; yet through it all she maintained a realistic, honest approach to her work and was never known to be difficult or hard to handle. Basically she was shy and needed frequent encouragement, for she never really believed in her own ability and her success was a source of never-ending wonder and amazement to her.

Perhaps the most stabilizing proof of her atypical image as an actress and off-screen wife and mother is that unlike many of her contemporaries she is not one of the oft-married personalities. Her first marriage ended in divorce, but since that time, she has been happily married to the same man for thirty years. Her name has not been linked with scandal, drugs, alcohol or psychiatric problems. It is also evident that she will not end her days in a home for destitute actors, being independently wealthy through a series of wise investments begun when she was a top star.

Unlike many of the greats to whom money became a curse or a deadly treadmill of trying to keep up with their own images, Alice did not think it necessary to entertain on a lavish scale or present a facade of unbounded affluence. While she has lived well, her tastes are surprisingly simple. She is still an avid bargain hunter, but generous to a fault both of her finances and her time when she is convinced of a worthy cause or recipient.

At the time of her appearance in WEEK-END IN HAVANA she was at the peak of her screen career. She would make but four more film appearances, and in 1945 she voluntarily retired to devote her time to her husband, orchestra leader Phil Harris, and raise her two daughters. At the time of her withdrawal from a screen career she was one of the top salaried stars at her home studio; her name on a theatre marquee was an automatic guarantee of capacity business. Her studio was deluged with thousands of anxious inquiries asking when Alice Faye would next appear on the screen. Properties were purchased with her in mind, writers turned out scripts designed especially for her, and the studio from time to time would announce that one of their upcoming productions would star her. Scripts were sent to her home, they were duly read and promptly returned, often with Alice's own notation as to whom she thought the lead role should go.

If she was not typical of other stars in her productive years she is even less typical of ex-stars today. In her home near Palm Springs she swims daily in her pool and exercises almost religiously. At fifty-six she appears younger than her years, and at five feet four, still weighing one-hundred twenty pounds, has the figure of a girl of twenty, and still conveys the warmth and sincerity movie audiences fondly remember. There is no need for her to rise before dawn, sit sleepily to be made up, and then carefully gowned, face a camera at nine in the morning and pretend to enjoy a rendezvous at a fashionable night spot. She entertains occasionally, has become a well-known figure in desert circles, visits her daughters, enjoys her four grandchildren and travels when the notion appeals to her. There are infrequent appearances on television, usually with her husband, which she does for the fun of it just to keep her finger in the pie.

She has few regrets about her life and her past as a picture star. She is honestly amazed at the interest shown by cinema groups for screenings of her films. "What do they see in those old pictures?" she inquired recently. "And why me of all people?"

The answer isn't a simple one of few words. Alice Faye, more than anyone else of her time projected a quality hard to analyze. Whether fortunately or unfortunately her screen roles, with one exception, were "good girl" parts. Her films more often than not were formula in that they focused on a backstage theme. It was often a thin theme of girl meets boy, a ripening awareness of love, career conflicts or another woman, the parting of the ways, and finally a reconciliation at the fadeout. Close examination of these films often finds Alice hurt and left alone to make her way. How many times did she turn the other cheek, sail away to London for a triumphant stage success, and then return to succor those who had wronged her? One gets the impression that the same hand wrote the stories, and they often did, while either Tyrone Power or John Payne brought her heartache and tears. In a recent informal discussion of her films it was noted that her leading men often made her cry. "Yes," she laughed with a hint of that old devilish twinkle, "but didn't I do it well?"

Through the shortcomings of story lines and the obvious inability of her leading men to see and appreciate her full worth at first glance, Faye projected a soft, feminine allure. She never screamed in rage or threw things. Instead she turned away and resolutely plotted her own course. If the tears flowed, and they usually did, the head was unbowed with firm resolve. Audiences suffered with her, and in so doing she became a real person, not just a screen image. Her male followers longed to comfort her and provide the love she found so elusive, while her female fans saw in her a woman who calmly could surmount the troubles at hand, and in so doing become stronger than the males in her life. But everyone from the inexperienced child to the octogenarian felt an overpowering gentle warmth of personality which seemed to envelope them individually.

It would be innacurate to classify Alice Faye as one of the screen's great beauties. She was not. The forehead was high, the nose upturned, the cheeks prominent and almost plump. Her detractors claimed the Faye chin was too long and jutted forward at an alarming angle. Others found distracting the slight mole-like imperfection on her upper lip. But everyone, even those that saw a somewhat "bovine-like quality" to her face, admitted that the Faye eyes were quite another matter. They were vividly blue, expressing the sincerity and honesty of their owner. Adorned with long, velvety lashes, they appeared from the screen like dipping ostrich plumes bent on caressing each member of the audience. It was the Faye eyes with their straightforward expressiveness which few could resist.

Like most stars of her time, Faye suffered from the all-too-common practice of trying to be made over in the image of another. When Alice reached the screen in 1934 Jean Harlow was riding a wave of popularity second to none. Each studio had a Harlow type, and at Fox Alice Faye became still another. It was an unfortunate mold and one which did not fit. Her hair was bleached almost white, her lips were accentuated into a thin almost hard line, and the plucked brows with the pencil-thin lines redrawn hardened her natural softness.

In addition, costume designers often dressed her in gowns which did nothing to flatter her figure. Even dismissing the trend of broad shoulders begun by Adrian and the wide, masculine lapels, Faye looked lost and out of place in such creations in SING, BABY, SING, WAKE UP AND LIVE and TAIL SPIN. Oddly enough, she claims today that she liked her clothes and thought them exciting at the time. She was undeniably at her best in period costumes such as those for LILLIAN RUSSELL or HELLO, FRISCO, HELLO, but the contemporary gowns of Travis Banton in THAT NIGHT IN RIO, and Gwen Wakeling's for WEEK-END IN HAVANA were among her best.

As a singing star Alice took a back seat to no one, and her studio quickly realized that when she was singing, activity by Alice or those about her was not in the best interests of the song or their star. The most vividly remembered songs by film goers today are those in which she stood perfectly still leaning either on a piano or against a door or pillar while the camera moved in for a closeup. Who can forget the heart-stirring "This Is Where I Came In" from SALLY, IRENE, AND MARY as she leans on the boat railing or sits in the doorway as the tears again roll down her cheeks; "Blue Lovebird" from LILLIAN RUSSELL in which she stands, never moving, against a black drape, or the immensely popular "You'll Never Know" from HELLO, FRISCO, HELLO sung into a telephone as she leans against a table?

Often while singing, Alice would be seen to curl or twist her lip slightly or audiences would notice a distinctive tremble. While appealing to some it was a quality which would come in for more than its share of adverse criticism. Frank Nugent writing in *The New York Times* on February 26, 1938, had this to say in his review of SALLY, IRENE, AND MARY. "Speaking personally, we've had enough close-ups of the luscious Miss Faye, whose inability to speak or sing without throwing her mouth into trembles has begun to wear us down." Three years later critic John Hobart writing in San Francisco noted in his WEEK-END IN HAVANA review, "As for Miss Faye, her eyes are blue and her hair is golden, which makes a nice color scheme on the screen, and her lower lip, in all honesty, quivers less than it usually does." If some critics found it disconcerting, the public as a whole felt it was merely distinctively Faye, and even Darryl F. Zanuck, in charge of production at Fox, admitted that, "No one can sell a song quite as well as Alice Faye."

Throughout her career Alice was fortunate to have as cameramen on her films such internationally famous cinematographers as: Karl Freund, Ernest Palmer, Arthur Miller, and Leon Shamroy. However, the staging of most musical sequences in Faye films was often less than outstanding in that these were often shot from

the audience straight onto a stage with few inventive angles. It was typically Fox too that settings tended to be conventionally static, offering even the best cameraman no opportunity for innovations. Performers played to the camera as to an audience. Warners and M-G-M went to the opposite extreme in making musical settings gigantic in proportion and excitingly original while the camera was an all-seeing eye from a vast variety of positions. Audiences were thus freed of a straight-on view of the proceedings. Thus the camera became a free-moving observer.

Another distinctive Faye-ism was her body stance. Whether by design or merely because it was a natural position is hard to say, but like the mouth tremble and the expressive eyes the position of the legs was usually the same. Countless stills give evidence of this only too well. She usually stood with weight supported on one leg, usually the left, knees together, and the right leg bent at the knee. Often only the toe of the right foot touched the floor for balance. This position showed up in her films repeatedly as well, notably in ALEXANDER'S RAGTIME BAND as well as most of her other films.

If her stance was distinctive, so was the Faye walk. When in a hurry, the shoulders were thrust forward. Thus with firm resolve, she moved forth with a no-nonsense air. You knew she meant business even if the tears suggested uncertainty, and the pouting lips offered something akin to ambiguity. In her lighter moments, Alice's movements, especially the unhurried gait, were entirely different from her fellow stars. As she progressed across a room in a slow, casual manner the shoulders came into play again, first one and then the other was swung forward. At no time was this better illustrated than in WEEK-END IN HAVANA, when leaving John Payne at the table in the Casino Madrilena, she made her way down a short flight of stairs to the dance floor. Stopping to survey some Cuban singers, she smiled in happy anticipation. Then, moving toward the entrance of the bar, the shoulders moved expressively, one hand nervously shook an orchid corsage and a chiffon handkerchief. From there she progressed to the moonlit terrace, but with her destination now uncertain the bravado began to slip away.

Probably no star of her time was to be so involved in screen stories with a radio background as Alice Faye. Five of her thirty-three scripts centered on broadcasting themes: EVERY NIGHT AT EIGHT, POOR LITTLE RICH GIRL, SING BABY SING, WAKE UP AND LIVE, and, of course, THE GREAT AMERICAN BROADCAST. In two other films she faced a mike briefly: in ALEXANDER'S RAGTIME BAND during the Carnegie Hall broadcast at that film's conclusion and her entire sequence as a guest star in FOUR JILLS IN A JEEP. But in between these were other stories which served to break up what might otherwise have become a monotonous pattern.

In most of her films it was the musical aspects which seemed to count most. Stories were adapted mainly with the purpose of spotlighting musical sequences at regular intervals. This in itself served to limit the scope, not to mention the depth of themes and story situations which could prevail. When judging the merits of such performers, and this applies to all stars whose singing voices or dancing feet were to be given full range, it must be remembered that the type of stories was automatically limited. Not many musical stories were laid in the out-of-doors, and the chance to develop innovations and new settings were held to a minimum. In Alice's case her numbers were showcased almost entirely in interior settings, and the few with out-door locales were usually on the decks of ships or ferry boats (STOWAWAY; SALLY, IRENE, AND MARY; TIN PAN ALLEY; and WEEK-END IN HAVANA). Thus to criticize the sameness or a degree of shallowness in her scripts is entirely unfair to Faye as to any musical star.

On the other hand it is also futile to speculate on what might have been had she demanded more original scripts or even approval of story and/or directors. During the years when she was working at 20th Century-Fox the pace was fast even for those days of casual movie making. Alice herself was so busy rehearsing and filming her current picture, making quick trips to wardrobe for fittings of dresses and costumes for her next screen assignment, and studying scripts that there wasn't time to make demands. Besides, who would listen to such demands in 1937? The studio system which prevailed had long-range plans which set up shooting schedules often two years in advance, and most of the major plants worked on a tight schedule resulting often in

one release a week. After her first year in Hollywood, Alice's films were all big budget productions. Shooting schedules were held to a strict pace and pressure on stars and directors alike was rigidly enforced.

It was not uncommon for a film to wrap up shooting before noon. Prior to lunch, final costume fittings for her next picture would take place, and in the afternoon Alice would be on a new set to begin shooting on the next film, the songs for which had already been recorded. This is not to say that Alice was overworked any more than any other star of her time. But it left little time for casual living between picture assignments. Even child stars like Shirley Temple and Jane Withers made four or five films a year, and Temple did seven her first year of feature film production.

Like all stars under contract to a major studio, Alice had a variety of directors — eighteen in all. They were men with varying backgrounds. Two were essentially dance directors: George White and Busby Berkeley; three were one-time actors: Raoul Walsh, Gregory Ratoff (who alternated between acting and directing through much of his career), and Jose Ferrer. Two of Faye's directors were acknowledged as among the greatest of Hollywood: Henry King and Otto Preminger. Alice credits Henry King as the one person responsible for giving her career its greatest boost as well as one of her most helpful, understanding and sympathetic mentors. "He's a great man, and one of Hollywood's finest talents. He gave me one of my biggest breaks, and I'll never forget him! Never!" There is evidence that King thought highly of Alice as well, for it was he who insisted she was right for Belle Fawcett in IN OLD CHICAGO. Of the remaining directors there were such skilled craftsmen as Irving Cummings, a four-time director of Faye films, whom she refers to as among her favorites and Walter Lang, William A. Seiter, and H. Bruce Humberstone, who directed some of her best pictures. At least one of the eighteen was to prove himself entirely unsympathetic to the talents of the Fair Faye. They worked together more than once, and it was a trying period for both. For Faye it was discouraging and one of the low periods of her career. She prefers to forget the whole experience. "It was a long time ago now," she recalled grimly. "Water under the bridge."

To examine Faye as a movie star, one needs first to examine the Faye background. Where did she begin, and what were the circumstances which led to a Hollywood career and the success as a super star during the Golden Age of the Movies?

She was born Alice Jeane Leppert in the Hell's Kitchen area of New York on May 5, 1915*. She traces her lineage to a Scotch, Irish, German and French ancestry. The family lived in a run-down tenement which was all that her father, Charley Leppert, could afford on his fourteen-dollar-a-week salary as a city patrolman. Alice was the youngest of three children and the only girl. From her earliest recollection there was always the necessity of counting every nickel and dime and worrying about the rent coming due all too soon. This undoubtedly had an effect upon the child who would one day still shop for bargains and be cautious about throwing her money around.

She attended Public School No. 84 at Sixth Avenue and Fifty-fourth Streets, where she was something of a tomboy eager to be noticed and not averse to shooting spit wads on a trusty rubber band. Even then she loved to dance and mimic, and at home was encouraged by Grandma Moffit, who lived with the family. But school held little excitement for her and, while she was a good student, she was not an outstanding one. At the age of thirteen she gave up further education and decided upon show business as a place in which to make her mark.

One spring night in 1927 she stood on a crowded sidewalk at the corner of Fifth Avenue and Fifty-ninth Street near an entrance to Central Park watching the tall towers of elegant hotels and town houses. She saw the lovely gowns of the wealthy, the revolving doors, and the big limousines. With a painful twinge of envy she resolved then and there that she'd have some of this richness and beauty. That she succeeded so well is no small tribute to a girl of twelve with a dream that life just somehow had to be better than it was.

She began to take dancing lessons, borrowing money from her brother Bill, who was by then working. If she grew discouraged there was always her soft-spoken mother offering encourage-

* Various reference books list 1912 as do mid-thirties fan magazines. Evidence seems to indicate the 1915 date is more accurate, however.

ment and Grandma Moffit telling her how good she was. Then suddenly, on her eightieth birthday, Grandma Moffit was dead. It was a stunning blow, one that Alice mistakenly attributed to the poverty she saw all about her.

With firm resolve she brazenly tried out for the Ziegfeld Follies at the tender age of thirteen. She looked older and much more sophisticated, and what was even better was selected, until in a moment of confusion she slipped and admitted to being thirteen. The casting director smiled and told her politely to go home.

"I want to make money," she insisted to her mother. "There's so little time, and I want to buy things and have things."

Her mother offered consolation. "You'll look fifteen, at least, in another year." The prophecy hadn't been one of a parent making idle conversation to bridge a difficult period.

Alice commenced singing lessons, but she proved to be a frustrating pupil to her teacher. She refused to learn music, knowing that she had only to hear a song once and she could sing it. "She won't listen to reason about music," her teacher complained to Mrs. Leppert. "She's got rhythm and a natural blues voice and that's enough."

It wasn't the natural voice which brought her the opportunity she longed for. At fifteen, her figure was one of a more mature girl. She tried out for a spot with the Chester Hale vaudeville unit, landed a dancing spot, and toured the eastern circuit for nearly three years playing an extended engagement at the Capitol Theatre. During these early years her future seemed to be in her feet; she danced well, and few even knew that she could sing.

It was about this time that she changed her name to Faye. Legend has it that the name was taken from Frank Fay, then a headline act in vaudeville. Not so claimed Alice. "I liked the name, and it went well with Alice. There was no attempt to copy or adopt anyone else's name. There wasn't much thought or planning behind it."

After several other chorus jobs Alice landed a spot in one of the best-known New York revues, GEORGE WHITE'S SCANDALS. It seemed like a tremendous step in the right direction for a young girl, and fame was just around the corner, but just what corner that was remained to be seen.

One evening at a party for members of the cast she was asked to participate in the cutting of a record just for fun. "But I don't know any speeches," she protested. When it was suggested she sing, she stepped to the mike, and with Rudy Vallee at the piano gave out with a rendition of "Mimi."

Unknown to her at the time an attorney friend of Rudy Vallee's named Hyman Bushel took the record home with him and played it next day for Vallee. He suggested that Rudy give Alice a chance on his radio show, for Vallee had been looking for a girl vocalist. Rudy was not sure. Alice lacked a name, but Bushel suggested that Vallee would have no trouble building Alice into a name.

So the Connecticut Yankee took a chance. For her first time on the air Alice, aged seventeen, sang "Honeymoon Hotel," and, as the notes died out at the song's conclusion, fainted dead away from sheer fright. Listeners, however, loved her and begged for more, but the Fleischmann sponsors were not impressed and refused a contract. Vallee, convinced by the listeners response, paid her salary from his own pocket, and she was launched as a regular on his program.

Alice at last seemed on her way to something important. Vallee and his orchestra had become one of the hottest orchestras in the country turning out hit after hit, cutting a series of records for the Victor label and playing such big New York night clubs as the Hollywood and the Pennsylvania Roof. At this time Alice made her first recording with Vallee singing "Honeymoon Hotel." Thus began a very successful recording career which would run until 1937.

Fate now took a hand in a rather ironic manner. Vallee took his radio show on an eastern tour. One evening while Alice was driving in Virginia with Vallee in a blinding storm, their car left the road and overturned. She was rushed to the hospital in a passing truck, and doctors worked valiantly on her cut face. Convinced that she'd be scarred for life and her career would be over almost before it began, Alice underwent three weeks of uncertainty. When the bandages were removed there was only a trace of a scar which the slight reworking of an eyebrow would carefully camouflage.

The three weeks had worked a minor miracle in still another way. While she had lain in the hospital fighting doubt and uncertainty, listeners

8   *From "She Learned About Sailors."*

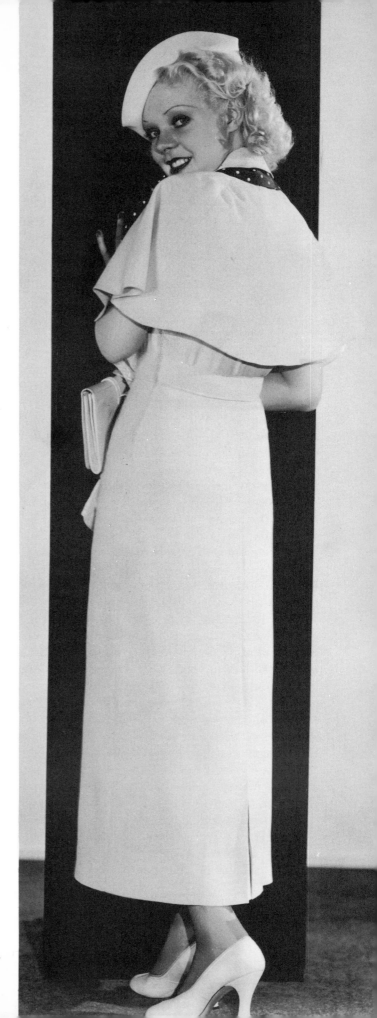

had swamped the sponsors of the show with inquiries as to the whereabouts of the lovely singer. Upon her return to the show, Alice was given a contract as a regular member of the broadcasting team.

Within a few months Vallee signed a new contract — Hollywood and a film version of GEORGE WHITE'S SCANDALS. Alice went along to the coast. It would be a six-weeks' vacation for her, she'd have a number in the film, and meanwhile the Fleischmann broadcasts continued.

Again fate stepped into the center ring providing Alice's big break, and another legend about her was told. Lilian Harvey, a blonde English born-German reared actress, had been assigned the SCANDALS lead opposite Vallee. Miss Harvey had starred in three Fox ventures, but neither she nor the studio had been entirely happy with the results. So the story goes, Lilian, unhappy about the size of her part, walked off the SCANDALS set and Faye, due to the urging of Vallee, was rushed in to replace her.

According to Alice, that version was not entirely true. She had already filmed her number, "Nasty Man," which was looked upon favorably. "Somehow I knew it was good," she said. "I was determined to be a star, and Sidney Kent, a wealthy backer of movie properties, said, 'Why not give the part to Alice Faye?'"

The studio did just that, but White, who had been given carte blanche on supervising every detail of this filmed version of his stage success, was at first not pleased. It was no small task for a complete movie unknown, only eighteen years old, to walk into a studio and take over a lead role intended for an international star. The overall results proved to be not only favorable, but GEORGE WHITE'S SCANDALS was a pronounced success, and the public and press began talking of a new Fox star. Star or not, Alice had been signed to a three-year contract. And much like the later movie script for A STAR IS BORN, Alice, the young star, rose rapidly in the east, while Vallee, her benefactor, saw his picture career slowly sinking over the western horizon.

The critics were generally favorable in praise of Alice; some preferring not to commit themselves with a wait-and-see reservation. When the second SCANDALS reached the screen the next year comparisons were in order, and some re-

viewers thought the first version somewhat bawdy and racy. Viewed today it is extremely tame, far from racy, and is merely a framework on which to hang almost a dozen musical numbers, some quaintly old-fashioned but extremely satisfying for a 1930's movie buff.

During this period the press worked overtime on the new Fox star, and some hinted openly of a romance with Vallee. There was no question that Alice exhibited an affection for Vallee, and she even had it written into her contract that shooting on her films would be suspended so that she might listen to his Thursday afternoon broadcasts. Alice had stated repeatedly that there was no romance between them, but not a few felt that the young actress had made no secret of her affections in such musical sequences in the picture as "Hold My Hand" or "Sweet and Simple."

But whatever their feelings for each other, it did not help matters when Fay Webb, Vallee's wife, sued him for divorce naming Alice as the reason for their marital discord. The attendant publicity was upsetting to Fox's new star, and as a result Alice was aware of a return of uncertainties about herself. Her shyness and dread of fan magazine interviews were duly recorded.

After the release of the SCANDALS there was nothing more for Vallee, never the strongest of leading men in film circles. Though he would act many times in films in the future and to extremely favorable acclaim, his roles would, for the most part, be character parts. As a result he departed Hollywood to continue working with his orchestra and fulfilling broadcasting engagements to which his unique personality was more favorably suited.

Fox now realized that Alice might prove to be a box-office draw of some magnitude, and she was rushed into NOW I'LL TELL BY MRS. ARNOLD ROTHSTEIN. The film advertising soon shortened the title to the first three words. The story of a well-known gambler starred Spencer Tracy in the lead role. Alice was Peggy Warren, his mistress. She was billed third under Helen Twelvetrees who played Tracy's long-suffering wife. Alice recalls being frightened by Tracy, a formidable star who was not always easy to know or communicate with. She sang one song and was violently killed in an auto crash. It was the only time she died in any screen role; even LILLIAN RUSSELL did not deal with that star's final years. Alice's part in NOW I'LL TELL was the smallest of her career, and while the critics were not especially kind, the exposure in a major dramatic hit did not hurt.

Immediately following, Faye was cast in two low-budget comedies with music. Both of these: SHE LEARNED ABOUT SAILORS and 365 NIGHTS IN HOLLYWOOD, were filmed at the old Fox studios in Hollywood. It seemed to her like a comedown after working in the larger studio near Beverly Hills, and again doubts crept in. Was the studio unhappy with her work? Was she going to be dropped quietly and her screen career terminated before it could move into high gear?

For a time after her arrival in Hollywood, Alice and her mother had lived in an apartment in the building owned by Mae West just a short distance from Paramount Studios in Hollywood. During that first year Alice realized a long-standing dream. She brought the whole family to the coast and took great delight in renting a large home complete with a patio and a pool.

Both of Alice's brothers quickly adopted the Faye name; Charles entered the picture industry as an assistant director, and William became her agent and handled her finances and business affairs, a position he still holds today in addition to a roster of other clients. He still maintains offices on Wilshire Boulevard in Beverly Hills.

In 1935 Charles Leppert returned to New York on a visit. Alice was in the midst of making a picture when informed that her father had been stricken and was in serious condition in a hospital. She abruptly left the studio, boarded a train for the east and helplessly watched the miles crawl by. Her father died before she reached New York and the press made much of the fact that he died in a charity ward of a public hospital. They had not troubled themselves to check into the matter further. Mr. Leppert had been taken to the first available hospital and no one had thought to ask for different accommodations. The incident did nothing to cement relations between Alice and the press, and served only to strengthen her natural shyness and reluctance to talk about herself.

If she had had doubts about her previous two picture assignments, the second filmed edition of the SCANDALS dispelled all of them. She

was top billed above James Dunn; *he* had received top billing in 365 NIGHTS IN HOLLYWOOD. Thus as the gloom of the depression deepened and Hollywood felt the pinch, Alice in her fifth screen appearance in a year became a star. GEORGE WHITE'S 1935 SCANDALS afforded her much more opportunity to display her vocal assets which had attracted much attention and on which much of the musical worth of this film depended.

Suddenly for the first time in her career there was nothing immediately ready for her at Fox and so the studio agreed to a Paramount loan-out. The result was Alice's first "radio" story, EVERY NIGHT AT EIGHT. Though she was starred with George Raft, it was newcomer Frances Langford who ended up with him at the final fadeout. Romantically Alice was left out in the cold; it was the last time she would work at Paramount.

Conditions at the Fox lot had grown steadily worse as the depression dragged on. The year 1935 was an especially trying period for all. There was talk of the studio closing down, rumors of bankruptcy, and ominous rumbles of massive personnel layoffs. What was actually taking place was a merger with 20th Century Pictures destined to become one of the leading major production centers for motion pictures in the world with branches in nearly every country in the world, a far-flung film empire impossible for anyone to foresee at that time.

Back at her own studio, Alice starred above Bebe Daniels in MUSIC IS MAGIC, but the better sequences featured Bebe. By the time of its release late in 1935 Faye's name on the marquee was commanding respect and a following of eager fans could be counted on to see each of her pictures. The merger now complete, MUSIC IS MAGIC was the first Faye film to bear the new 20th Century-Fox trademark.

Before the year was out Alice was at work with Warner Baxter and Jack Oakie in KING OF BURLESQUE, a musical which she would refilm again in 1943 under the title of HELLO, FRISCO, HELLO. The latter film was one of her greatest hits, but with KING OF BURLESQUE she was starred in one of the studio's most important musicals to start the new year of 1936.

The year 1936 was something of a turning point in Alice's career. She had become a star in her first year in Hollywood, but she was still sporting the artificial Harlow look and would again in her next film, the first of two Shirley Temple films she made that year. It is somewhat ironic that Shirley had appeared briefly in NOW I'LL TELL playing one short sequence of four lines. Known as the mortgage raiser at Fox, Temple was the studio's biggest single asset following the death of Will Rogers. It was now Alice who appeared in support of Temple. It was an association she did not find entirely satisfactory. That Shirley was a bright child and a whiz of efficiency no one could deny, but most adult stars disliked assignments in Temple pictures. Scripts were tailored entirely for Shirley, and for a Barrymore, a Cooper, or a fast-rising young star like Faye there was just too much of Temple for good measure. But exposure in a Temple film was international exposure, and that kind of thing could only mean more of a following.

It is interesting that in POOR LITTLE RICH GIRL a young singer named Anthony Martin was seen briefly as a radio crooner. More would be heard from him shortly.

For her role of Joan Warren in SING, BABY, SING Alice cast off forever the brashness of her Harlow period and in its place was substituted the more natural softness which would be her stock in trade for the remainder of her screen career. It was on the set of this picture that Alice and Martin met for the first time. He had, at first, been reluctant about approaching her and asking for a date. After all she was a big star, and he was a supporting player on the way up. To his surprise Alice agreed, and they began to see each other socially.

It was during the early filming of this picture that Alice took note of a young hopeful about Hollywood. He had appeared as an extra in two films at other studios. So convinced was she that he was star material that she asked the studio to test him, and even appeared in that test with him. The studio was impressed, and he was signed to a contract. Alice was hopeful that he would be cast opposite her in SING, BABY, SING, and the studio had at first agreed. But the strikingly handsome Tyrone Power wasn't a name in pictures though his father had made some inroads in the early talkies. Stills for this production were even printed and exist today which bear his name at the lowest point of billing: Tyrone Power, Jr. Michael Whalen was given the part instead. It is often said that the worm turns. Power, within a few short months, shot to the top as one of Hollywood's brightest stars, while Whalen slipped quickly into a string of insignificant B's and was ultimately phased out of a film career entirely.

At the conclusion of SING, BABY, SING the studio was so delighted with Alice's work that her old contract was torn up and a new one written. The little girl from Tenth Avenue was on her way.

Temple again starred in STOWAWAY, but Alice fared better in regard to footage in the finished film than she had in the former Temple vehicle. There was a romantic chance for her as well in that she was given Robert Young as costar, and their scenes together were well played. Competing with Young for her favors was Allan Lane, a young actor who would star in a profitable string of western films, and Helen Westley gave one of her bright, animated performances as Lane's meddling mother. Alice took third billing in this as well as her next, ON THE AVENUE, her first film to boast a score by Irving Berlin.

ON THE AVENUE had almost everything that a good musical film should possess. In addition to Berlin's standout songs, the studio borrowed Warner's Dick Powell, and in the cast was the lovely Madeleine Carroll, one of the screen's great beauties. If the Ritz Brothers wore a bit thin as had the earlier antics of Mitchell and Durant in three Faye films, audiences loved their clowning. It was one of the year's biggest money makers, but in it Alice again lost her man — this time to Carroll.

Berlin was pleased with the way Alice sang his songs. Now those within the industry were coming in for their share of praise of Alice Faye as a screen personality. Though she was rushed from one film to the next, often with little or no time off between, Alice often doubted her own ability and could not believe in the praise that came her way. In an interview for a fan magazine in 1937 Alice admitted, "I still have an awful feeling of doubt, but it doesn't petrify me as it once did. I do as well as I can and I constantly try to improve my work, and that's about all that anyone can do."

WAKE UP AND LIVE followed immediately, and historians in cinema circles still regard it as one of the best satires on radio that Hollywood ever produced. It was not one of Alice's favorite films, and was one that underwent judicious cutting by the time it reached release. It was more Jack Haley's film than Alice's, with Walter Winchell and Ben Bernie given top billing though neither was an actor. They did come across in a relaxed, natural fashion, but in England, at any rate, Alice Faye and Jack Haley were given top billing, for the feud between the two radio personalities had no meaning there.

Alice and Tony were now spending quite a bit of off-screen time together. They sought out interesting places to dine, took drives to Malibu, and were delighted when Tony was cast in Alice's next film, YOU CAN'T HAVE EVERYTHING. Meanwhile still another new contract had been negotiated for her by the studio.

The year 1937 might very well be known as the most eventful as well as busy year for 20th Century-Fox's fast-rising Alice Faye. No sooner had WAKE UP AND LIVE been completed than she was again at work on YOU CAN'T HAVE EVERYTHING, a script fashioned especially for her. It was the first film in which Alice would costar with Don Ameche.

During the making of the film the script called for her to consume a plate of spaghetti, then, hunger not abated, order still another. By the time the scene had been done to the director's satisfaction Alice could hardly stand the sight of the stuff. That evening, dining at the home of a friend, what was she served as a gag? Spaghetti! No one detected the slightest hint of her previous experiences of the day, for Alice downed it without a word.

As summer wore on the rumors of marriage grew stronger, some people openly insisted that Alice and Tony were wed or certainly about to be. One Friday evening when she and Tony attended the fights at the Stadium she had dressed in pale blue, a perfect bridal outfit. As they entered the Brown Derby for dinner songwriter Lew Pollock, just for a gag, spread the word, "They're married." Alice and Tony were eating when Walter Winchell hurried up to excitedly berate Alice for not giving him an exclusive on her marriage.

At one time or another they disagreed and parted company for short periods. When YOU CAN'T HAVE EVERYTHING was given a spe-cial preview at the Alexander Theatre in Glendale on June twenty-third, the studio was delighted with the audience reaction.

Though she had been living with her brother Bill in Beverly Hills, Alice longed for a home of her own. Before she could seriously house-hunt, her career took another upsurge when the studio undertook one of their most costly productions based upon the story of the O'Leary family and the cow which started the historic conflagration. Henry King, the project's director, insisted on testing Alice for the part of Belle, a role tailored for Jean Harlow, whom Fox hoped to get on loan-out from M-G-M. Harlow's death in June set King to thinking that Alice would be ideal for the part, and he arranged a special test. The studio wasn't sure, but King was convinced when he saw the test, and the studio agreed. Tyrone Power, now a full-fledged star welcomed the news, for he often said that Alice did more for his career than anyone by openly being a champion of his cause in his bid for a screen career. The picture was in production for many months, but Alice's part, though second only to Power's, was more quickly filmed. It was a project the public would not see until nearly the middle of 1938.

In the meantime Alice was loaned to Universal for YOU'RE A SWEETHEART, which began under the working title of YOUNG MAN'S FANCY. The music was right, the gowns for Alice excellent, and she enjoyed the top-star treatment of the assignment. Never known as a top screen dancer, she was given two such numbers with costar George Murphy, and "So It's Love" was her best screen number to that time.

Though Alice had refused to admit publicly that she would actually marry Tony Martin, friends knew that she was deeply in love with him. She half-heartedly claimed that "conflicting careers" would prevent their marriage. Perhaps she subconsciously knew this would be true, but rumors not withstanding, Alice requested a day off from shooting at Universal, and in Yuma, Arizona, she became Mrs. Tony Martin on September fourth.

Happy to cash in on the publicity, the studio rushed them both into SALLY, IRENE, AND MARY, a backstage story with a few novel twists, the clowning of Joan Davis, and the haughty, imperious grandeur of Louise Hovick, i.e., Gypsy Rose Lee. Fred Allen and Jimmy

Durante came in for a share of the pie, and the company was a happy one.

When Jack Haley and his wife decided to sell their San Fernando Valley home just a short distance from the ranch of Clark Gable, Alice decided it was the ideal home for her. She bought the property and was delighted to be a home owner with its attendant domesticity. She had said often enough that what she wanted most was to have several children. Children and a home of her own.

In the meantime Alice plunged into work on ALEXANDER'S RAGTIME BAND, again with Ty Power. It soon became clear that their torrid love scenes in IN OLD CHICAGO had not been mere chance. They came across as one of the most potent screen teams of the decade. Again there was Berlin supplying the music and Alice to introduce the lovely "Now It Can Be Told." The huge cast under Henry King's professional direction gave outstanding performances down to the smallest bit, and then came the task of trimming the footage to a running time suitable for double billing in theatres. On May 21, 1938, the preview at the Cathay Circle Theatre drew an ovation, and praise was heaped upon the principals and the studio as well. BAND became one of the outstanding box-office attractions of the year, breaking records everywhere.

By this time IN OLD CHICAGO had been released, and the two films made almost every list of the ten best for 1938. Alice rode the crest of a wave of popularity such as she had never known before. It became difficult for her to shop in department stores, crowds recognized her everywhere she went, and while it did much to bolster her always sagging lack of confidence there were drawbacks as well. Audiences expected another CHICAGO or RAGTIME BAND role to follow, but two such outstanding films in a row did not guarantee that another would be forthcoming. It was the old story of a top star trying to get the best parts and being thrown a curve in the form of an old-fashioned pot boiler.

In this case the production was THE GIRL FROM BROOKLYN which began shooting in 1938. The script was at best vague, lacking characterization and depth. It was to be a semi-dramatic role, but after shooting had been in progress for some weeks, morale on the part of cast and crew began to deteriorate. It wasn't long before no one believed in what they were

With Edwin Burke, director of "Now I'll Tell."

doing. Gregory Ratoff, never the most prominent of directors, seemed to be getting nowhere, shooting lagged, and finally the project was abandoned.

Never idle for long, Alice was cast in another role which was an entirely different approach for her. This was the Frank Wead script of TAIL SPIN, a yarn about women fliers, and Roy del Ruth was the director in charge who had done so well with ON THE AVENUE two years before. If her previous project had languished and come to nothing, this shooting schedule was a marvel of speed and efficiency. Alice, Connie Bennett, and Nancy Kelly became daredevil aviators in a story of crashes, disasters, and disappointments without once leaving the ground. TAIL SPIN, released shortly after the start of 1939, did well at the box office, but it wasn't a typical Faye film though she did manage one song in the proceedings. The shapeless flying suits were hardly becoming; the loyal audiences expected her in chic gowns which were more in keeping with her now established image of a very feminine star.

Alice and Tony began 1939 with high hopes. Alice was now starring in ROSE OF WASHINGTON SQUARE, again under the direction of Ratoff, and Tony was working with Gloria Stuart in WINNER TAKE ALL. But an all-too-obvious fact was seen in the disparity of their respective careers. Alice was at the top, one of the biggest stars at 20th Century-Fox, with an impressive following and all her films were top-budgeted productions. Tony, however, wasn't the draw in pictures, and his assignments reflected this fact. He had fewer roles, less important pictures, and a career which was simply not getting anywhere. The old conflict of careers which Alice had spoken of almost hesitantly before their marriage was upon them with a vengeance, though maybe not in quite the same way she had previously feared. As a singer Tony had club dates to fulfill. It was a realm in which he was known and appreciated. So his work took him more and more away from home. At best it was not a happy situation.

If her personal life wasn't all that she might have wished it to be, Alice at least put up a good front. The studio had a new property ready for her, an exciting production entitled FALLING STARS. Again Irving Cummings would direct, Don Ameche would be her costar and, most exciting of all, the picture was to be filmed in Technicolor. It was an original story, and a role which was a distinct departure for a musical star. Alice acted a straight part with no songs, and this time the public didn't mind. The story was alive and its theme of the early days of film making in Hollywood suited Alice. Before release the title underwent a change and emerged as HOLLYWOOD CAVALCADE. The effect was almost electric. Alice was a revelation in Technicolor, the blue eyes their most exciting due to the fine camera work of Ernest Palmer. Technicolor in 1939 was usually shockingly garish, unrealistic, but a delight for the eye. Here it was muted and pleasingly subdued. Critics and public alike approved the non-singing Faye and the picture immediately ran up impressive grosses. Alice's own personal star had never been higher.

Throughout 1938 various rewrite jobs had been undertaken on the uncompleted THE GIRL FROM BROOKLYN, whose title was now changed to BY THE DAWN'S EARLY LIGHT. Alice was called back for retakes, but the time lapse had taken its toll. Her scenes at this time seemed disjointed at best and didn't make much sense to her, and there was always a new sequence being turned out by the writers. Again a title change was instituted. It was retitled WHITE LADY OF THE ORIENT, and the studio even printed stills with that title. More rewrites, more retakes, and once again the project was shelved.

During a brief lull between pictures Alice and Tony sailed for Honolulu for a holiday away from the activity of Hollywood. Columnists hinted that it was a belated honeymoon, an attempt to save a marriage already floundering hopelessly. The trip was a pleasant change, but both Alice and Tony were finding it hard to live with much privacy. Also the constant references in newspapers and fan magazines to a possible breakup had become as frantic as the rumors of marriage had been two years before. Tony was piqued at the references to him as Mr. Faye, and his film career wasn't going well. In 1939 he was dropped by 20th Century-Fox, though for a time both he and Alice were at work concurrently on films at different studios. Alice was making another period piece with Fred MacMurray and Richard Greene entitled LITTLE OLD NEW YORK, and at Columbia Tony starred with Rita Hayworth in MUSIC IN MY HEART.

From "On the Avenue."

Unhappy with her personal life, Alice plunged into her role of Pat O'Day, a barmaid on the waterfront of 1807 New York, under the direction of her old friend, Henry King. She felt at home in the part, and she and King worked well together. Alice sang only in a crowded scene with a group of dancing extras, but she handled a comedy part with sagacity and elan.

By this time WHITE LADY OF THE ORIENT was again before her. In late 1939 the film had been patched together and released under the title of BARRICADE. Alice had begged the studio to scrap the footage entirely, to start over, but the outlay on the production had been extensive, and the studio was eager to recoup what would otherwise have been a total loss. The critics were unanimous in panning the picture and Alice's acting fared little better, a situation entirely attributed to the script's inadequacies. The film reached completion with the screenplay credited to Granville Walker, in all probability a pseudonym for a variety of different writers.

Twentieth now had another big production for Alice, an ambitious screen biography of the great beauty of the nineties, LILLIAN RUSSELL. There was never any question as to whom the title role would go. Alice was ideally suited to the part, but though the cast was entrusted to capable actors, and Alice's old friend, Irving Cummings directed, the script wasn't top notch. Technicolor would have been a tremendous

asset, but the decision was made to shoot in black and white. Sets and costumes showed that no expense had been spared to make the production one of the studio's most impressive of the year. Alice admits it was a hard shooting schedule and a long one. She still regards LILLIAN RUSSELL as her most demanding role.

Like most stars of her day, Alice's contract now provided for a working year of roughly forty weeks. Shooting schedules, though less hurried than today, were roughly six weeks in length. Music productions ran somewhat longer, anywhere from seven to ten weeks depending upon the length of the finished film. Many stars preferred to work straight through for forty weeks and have a lay-off at the end, but this was not always possible on musical films.

Production now commenced on the first of a series of gay Latin-American themes to be filmed in color. DOWN ARGENTINE WAY would team Alice with Don Ameche once again, but a sudden attack of appendicitis put Alice in the hospital. A decision was quickly reached to replace her. The problem was, with whom? Someone remembered a blonde who had worked in Paramount musicals playing minor roles. Betty Grable had gone to New York where she had achieved success on the stage in the musical, DUBARRY WAS A LADY. She was quickly brought to the coast and rushed into the Faye role. Her rise was swift from that point on.

Film historians through the years have been quick to point out that it was Grable who "replaced" Faye and ultimately Monroe who "replaced" Grable. A closer examination of the facts proves that both Grable and Faye projected quite a different personality from the screen. DOWN ARGENTINE WAY was changed to fit the Grable temperament of a more extroverted blonde and to concentrate on her natural talents for dancing. In all fairness one cannot claim that Monroe "replaced" Grable. Their styles were markedly different. Grable was bright, breezy, bold, and brash. Monroe was a smoldering sexpot, a unique personality not essentially a singer like Faye nor a dancer like Grable. Comparisons between the three are thus unwarranted and entirely unfair to any of the trio of ladies in question.

By early 1940 it was obvious that the Faye-Martin marriage was over. Tony's career in films, always an uncertain entity, seemed to be getting nowhere. He became more and more in demand on the night-club circuit which, of course, took him away from Hollywood for much of the year. "It was no one's fault," Alice admitted. "We were always apart. I had to send him telegrams to communicate with him." Bitterly disillusioned by the breakup of her marriage, for she had been sincerely in love with her husband, Alice and Tony separated and were divorced that year.

After a period of recuperation from her operation, Alice returned to the studio for TIN PAN ALLEY. Casting difficulties arose almost at once. The project originally called for Ty Power and Don Ameche to costar with Alice, but conflicting film assignments made them unavailable. The script underwent revisions, a sister role was added for Betty Grable, and Jack Oakie and John Payne were brought in as the male leads.

Much has been made of a feud between Alice and Betty, for cynics were quick to point out that they never worked together again. Not so. Alice and Betty were always the best of friends both on screen and off. "We've remained good friends to this day," Alice confessed recently. "When I'm in Las Vegas I always visit her, and we enjoy each other's company. All that talk of dissent and career jealousies is just a lot of nonsense. I suppose it was good publicity, but it just wasn't true." It was the kind of story that sold movie tickets and had been heard since the days of the Gloria Swanson-Pola Negri dispute or that involving Bette Davis and Miriam Hopkins.

TIN PAN ALLEY remains one of the most musical Faye films and a vastly satisfying one. Alice again sailed off for London and stardom wearing a broken heart on her sleeve. Formula it may have been, but if she had ever lacked confidence and self-assurance it did not show from the screen. She was poised, warmly vibrant, and completely in control of her emotions.

As events later proved, Fox's DOWN ARGENTINE WAY was the forerunner of a frothy trilogy of Technicolored screen plays to reach the screen prior to World War II which glorified Pan-American relations. Alice headed the second of these begun as THE ROAD TO RIO and for obvious reasons quickly changed to THAT NIGHT IN RIO. Don Ameche was her husband

again; it was their sixth and last screen appearance together since they costarred in YOU CAN'T HAVE EVERYTHING four years before. To this day she regards Ameche as one of her best friends from her picture-making days. For years they participated in a series of running practical jokes and gags. She once sent him a pair of boxing gloves filled with blue forget-me-nots. In her final musical in 1943 she had a special line added in which she took a poke at her favorite costar. "Stop acting like Don Ameche and get me a cab!" she barked at James Ellison.

It was during the shooting of RIO that Alice met the man who would have such a decisive influence on her future life and ultimately her film career itself. At Charley Foy's Supper Club it was actor Jack Oakie who introduced Alice to orchestra leader Phil Harris. When they began to be seen in public the columnists made much of a new romance. This time the pronouncements came in the form of warnings. It wasn't wise, one said bluntly. Others hinted at differences in backgrounds, career conflicts would surely pull them asunder, while others openly suggested Alice was merely substituting one musical personality for another.

When shooting began on THE GREAT AMERICAN BROADCAST, her co-workers couldn't help but notice that it was a more relaxed, cheerful and confident Alice Faye facing the cameras. Payne and Oakie were again her costars, and again Payne caused the tears to flow freely, while the music poured forth just as freely. Several critics referred to BROADCAST as the best musical since ALEXANDER'S RAGTIME BAND.

On May 12, 1941, just three days after the release of THE GREAT AMERICAN BROADCAST, Alice and Phil were married in Mexico. The news was greeted with much shaking of heads and no little skepticism. Gossip columnists were sure both had made a grave error, and many openly gave the union six months at best. In less than six months, on September twentieth, they were remarried in Galveston, Texas. As of this writing the Faye-Harris marriage is clearly "working," and after thirty years it gives every indication of remaining on very firm ground indeed.

While working on her next film, WEEK-END IN HAVANA, another jaunt to the tropics by way of studio expertise and know-how, Alice announced she was expecting a child the next May. This final production of Twentieth Century-Fox's south-of-the-border trilogy was the first of three films in a row that Alice would film in Technicolor. It had everything going for it, and if the story was somewhat uncomplicated it had just the proper amount of "pizazz" as Pauline Kael would say to keep it rushing along at a most pleasing clip, ringing a happy sound at the nation's box offices.

The announcement that motherhood on the immediate horizon would necessitate Alice's withdrawal from films for a number of months caused consternation at Fox. Three scripts were in the planning stages as the next Faye pictures. Ginger Rogers was a proper bird-brained ROXIE HART; on loan from Columbia, Rita Hayworth became MY GAL SAL; while Betty Grable trouped off with John Payne and Carmen Miranda for a SPRINGTIME IN THE ROCKIES.

Thus for the first time since she came to Hollywood in 1934 to begin her picture career, a year was to pass with no new Faye film in release. On May nineteenth just two weeks after her twenty-seventh birthday Alice gave birth to a daughter who was named Alice Jr.

Shortly after the first of the year 1943, Alice returned to the studio for an elaborate Technicolor production entitled HELLO, FRISCO, HELLO. The story was in essence merely a reworking of Alice's first film of 1936, KING OF BURLESQUE. It was to find both Alice and Jack Oakie reenacting their original roles, with John Payne in the Warner Baxter part. H. Bruce Humberstone directed; he had worked previously on a Faye film in 1937 when he served as director of special effects (the fire sequences) on IN OLD CHICAGO.

Upon its release in March the response at the box office was unprecedented. In almost all of its original play dates in larger cities the run was extended, and the new Gordon-Warren song, "You'll Never Know," swept the country almost overnight. Alice was extremely pleased with the film and refers to it as one of her favorite screen appearances ranking alongside ALEXANDER'S RAGTIME BAND.

Fox was impressed with the returns on HELLO, FRISCO, HELLO. Realizing that the Faye name, especially in big-budget musicals, was money in the bank, the studio had yet another Technicolor musical ready to go. Production began on THE GANG'S ALL HERE under the direction of Busby Berkeley. It was to be the final musical in Alice's career as a top star, for during the production Alice found that she was again expecting a child. It was a long shooting schedule, and did not profit by tight direction. Berkeley was second to none in his complicated and intricate musical production numbers, but his direction of comedy or dramatic sequences was pedestrian and lackadaisical. With a becoming upswept hairdo in part of the film, Alice looked refreshingly lovely, and the vivid colors were a decided asset to accentuate her blue eyes. However, in portions of the film she seemed weary and almost bored.

If the production itself was not up to some of its predecessors, the grosses did not reflect this fact. Released at the end of 1943, it was one of the top-drawing films of early 1944.

Once again Alice was away from the cameras throughout 1944, though in March her guest spot in 4 JILLS IN A JEEP drew favorable response as she reprised her top song hit of 1943, "You'll Never Know." On April 26, 1944, Alice's second daughter, Phyllis, was born.

A new project loomed at Fox in which Faye and Grable would be reunited. But Alice was convinced of one thing, she did not want to do another musical right away. Thus when THE DOLLY SISTERS went into production Grable and June Haver costarred. The latter had appeared on the screen for the first time in 1943 playing a bit in Alice's THE GANG'S ALL HERE.

Alice meanwhile asked a change-of-pace for her next film and began reading scripts. None seemed to her entirely right. Then she learned of a new script which would be directed by Otto Preminger and would feature Dana Andrews. The two had worked together in one of 1944's best mystery yarns, and LAURA was one of the season's most talked-about productions. Confident that FALLEN ANGEL would be another LAURA, Alice asked for and was given the role of June Mills.

Things went well, and Alice found working with Dana Andrews pleasant. Even Preminger, the horrible Hun, held no terrors for her and they got on well. Somewhere along the line the word was put out to build up the Linda Darnell role. Once finished, the print was edited and a work print put together. Alice was present at the studio for a special screening of the film. "I was horrified at what they had done to it," she confessed. "My character was so changed from what the original script had called for. My song was entirely edited out." The song itself had taken almost a week to film. Together with Andrews in the car Alice had sung, "Slowly" on the way to the beach. Following it was a dramatic encounter between them in which Andrews slapped her. Many of her most telling scenes had ended up "on the cutting-room floor." The character came across as two-dimensional and rather passive.

Convinced that the film would be a failure, Alice made an exit from the studio that would have done credit to the most dramatic of movie scripts. Hurt and sure that her career would suffer as a result of FALLEN ANGEL, she ran to her car, climbed in and drove off. She did not even return to get her personal belongings in her dressing room. At the gate she tossed her keys to the guard and roared off destined not to return for sixteen years.

Perhaps behind all of this was a determination to make her marriage to Phil Harris work for all the reasons that the first had failed. Harris was and is a top-notch performer on the nightclub circuit, constantly in demand for guest appearances on television both here and in London. His work takes him away from home, often for many weeks at a time. Alice had had a most successful career as a picture star, there was really no reason for her to continue to work. She enjoyed her home and family and this in itself was reason enough to quit while she was still in demand, still at the top. Wouldn't it, then, be better for one career in the family to be quite enough? Evidently she thought so, and within a few months a new phase of her career would blossom. It would be far less demanding than a picture career.

It may come as a surprise to some, but Phil Harris is not all that he seems at first glance. Through the years the image he has chosen to project to the public is that of a philandering lush more interested in high living and making a game of life in which all the conventions are badly bent if not outright shattered. Harris is a methodical business man with a shrewd concept of giving the public what it wants. Like Dean Martin he plays up the drinking idea for all it is worth — it is merely expedient for his show business image. Away from his club and television audiences he is a devoted husband and father. His conduct is such that he need never be afraid to be anywhere at any time with anyone. He would be at home before royalty or in a Basin Street jazz joint. On a recent trip to England with his two daughters, people were surprised and enchanted by his interest in British historical spots. He spread good will wherever he went and was a gentleman possessed of charm, tact, and diplomacy.

At the time of her retirement she was a top-salaried star and had just signed a contract for two pictures a year, a forty-week work schedule which would pay her $200,000 a year. But even the best of scripts could not lure her back.

Periodically the studio, acting under the pressure of ardent requests from the exhibitors and public alike, announced her return. She was said to be returning to the screen as Aunt Cissy in A TREE GROWS IN BROOKLYN. Alice said no, and the role went to Joan Blondell. There was talk of starring her in THE RAZOR'S EDGE, a move which would reunite her with Tyrone Power. Again she turned it down.

If she had turned her back on a picture career another loomed on the horizon — radio. In the fall of 1946 Alice and Phil signed with Rexall for a weekly radio show which was aired on Sunday nights. The show was received with favor by listeners throughout the country, and THE PHIL HARRIS-ALICE FAYE SHOW occupied one of the prime air times (Sunday evenings) for a run which would continue until April of 1954.

Still the studio tried to lure her back with such properties as A LETTER TO FIVE WIVES (it became three wives in final release), THE HOUSE IN THE SQUARE (released as I'LL NEVER FORGET YOU) which was a Ty Power script of no little confusion, and even as late as 1950 she was asked to do WABASH AVENUE. Had she appeared in this latter production she would have played on screen with her real-life husband, Phil Harris.

During the years of THE PHIL HARRIS-ALICE FAYE SHOW she was able to remain in the entertainment world and still devote most of her time to her growing daughters. Certainly it is

Mr. and Mrs. Phil Harris

to her credit that her first thought was for her family, and it can never be said that the demands of a busy career left her little time for her children. The results paid off in the long run. Her daughters have grown into lovely young women now married and with children of their own. Their close-knit warm family atmosphere prevails to this day, and both Alice and Phil adore their four grandchildren.

In 1959 Alice appeared on television in THE PHIL HARRIS SHOW singing the songs that had made her famous in motion pictures. The response was gratifying, but she seemed unwilling to repeat the assignment at the time. Gradually, however, there were other television appearances which in the 60's became more frequent. Her reception on THE HOLLYWOOD PALACE, KRAFT MUSIC HALL, THE PERRY COMO SHOW and others brought out a frenzied group of her loyal fans.

In 1961 Alice let it be known that if the proper script could be found, and if the role was suitable to her age (then 46) she would consider returning to films. It was not a promise of a new career, but undoubtedly she wanted to see if she

was still remembered. The production of STATE FAIR proved to be merely another remake. It was spoken of as a comeback in many circles, and her performance as Melissa Frake was one of the script's more refreshing moments of which there were all too few.

"I do pretty much as I like now," she admits cheerfully. But if exotic climes seem to beckon, home looks best. She is seldom away from her home in the desert for more than a few weeks each year.

This past spring her appearance in New York brought out crowds eager to welcome her as *Liberty* magazine's "Star to Remember." She attended a performance of NO, NO NANETTE, and has publicly admitted that she would like to do the Ruby Keeler role on the west coast or in London. As of this writing no firm decision has been reached.

Her reactions to a career which has spanned almost forty years of stage, screen, radio, and television is still one of humble sincerity.

This can best be illustrated when, some years ago, she was interviewed by a Canadian radio station. The question put to her was this: "What was it like being the queen of one of the biggest - - ?" "Oh, just a minute," she broke in. "I never at any time ever considered myself the queen of anything. I was merely a part of a very large studio, doing a job the best way I knew how." When asked if it was a good life, one could almost see the twinkle in the soft, blue eyes and imagine the smiling lips as she replied, "I was so fortunate. I worked with some of the greatest people in the business. It was like a big family really. Time and again the same people worked on my pictures — the people behind the scenes were all wonderful to me, and I'll never forget them. But picture making has changed so much. I'm not sure I'd want to go back again. And what would I do now? Who'd want me now?"

Who indeed! The followers are as loyal as ever as evidenced by revivals of her films and repeated showings on television which have brought her legions of new fans. But whether or not Alice Faye returns to a career in pictures isn't terribly important at this point.

We knew and loved her when she *was* a queen at the pinnacle of a glittering career, and we love her still. One of her own songs says it so much more eloquently, "You'll never know just how much we miss you!"

FAIR FAYE— THE ENGLISH FAVORITE

by Arthur Nicholson

Alice Faye was as undeniably American as Anna Neagle was English. So how come the English, while acknowledging the talents of Miss Neagle and other English stars — all fell madly in love with the Fair Faye?

From her early days in the movies — even in 1935 — the English reviewers and picturegoers were falling under the Faye spell. They said — "She looks like Jean Harlow — but has a warmth under the sheen that Harlow lacks — *and* she can sing!! By the time she appeared in Shirley Temple's POOR LITTLE RICH GIRL in which she was beginning to lose her "Harlow" sheen and develop her own style and personality — the critics were cheering! And when SING, BABY, SING and ON THE AVENUE reached us — the transformation was complete! Alice captured all hearts with her warm, friendly, naturalness. Those hearts she captured she *still* holds today — the British are loyal to those they love! Her charming acting and — above all — her honey coated voice, made box office hits of all her 1936-1937 films.

Of course there were critics who still didn't care for some of her mannerisms — such as wrinkling her nose and curling her lips whilst singing — the same critics didn't care for Bette Davis's mannerisms or Garbo's aloofness — so Alice was in great company!! But Mr. and Mrs. Average England — didn't care. By then Alice was everyone's favorite daughter, or girl friend — and she could do no wrong.

Her special appeal to us was the fact that she *was* "sweet," and "nice" and "natural" without being cloying with it — luckily she could sing too! She made no pretentions to glamour and in those days her costumes were all sort of "girl next doorish" — other American stars of that era seemed to English eyes to be so remote and fabulous — Garbo with her mystery and classic tragedies! Bette Davis lashing everyone with forked tongue! Carole Lombard — so brittle! Those perennial working girls — Joan Crawford and Babs Stanwyck going from Macy's bargain basement to Adrian's Salon and Fifth Avenue Society — usually via a husband — or somebody else's. But with them we *knew* they were acting — but with Alice — like Ginger Rogers at that time — she was just being herself!

Pretty soon little Alice reached the "big time" in movies — when IN OLD CHICAGO and ALEXANDER'S RAGTIME BAND reached us — we were glad to see her wearing glamourous gowns and have becoming hairdos *and* handsome leading men. We were happy for her — just as we would have been if it had been our big sister making good! Usually in the 30's cinemas in England — programmes changed every three days — with special one night only films on Sundays (usually old ones). Only "special" films played all the week. CHICAGO and BAND were in that class — and from then on *all* Alice's films were "all the week" films! After we'd all cried with her — be-moaning her loss of Ty Power in BAND — Alice could do no wrong. The English are very sentimental — they love to cry! Alice was the *only* star who could bring tears with a song! Oh yes — there were other singers, and maybe bigger musicals! Miss MacDonald could trill her way through falling blossoms into Mr. Eddy's arms — Miss Garland would come later to tear at our nerves and set our senses tingling — but the public flocked to the Faye films — she played straight to the heart string with no nonsense about it!

We weren't *too* happy at TAIL SPIN because those other ladies, Miss Bennett and Miss Kelly, took up too much screen time from our Alice. Besides, how could Kane Richmond prefer Caustic Connie to Alluring Alice?? We adored ROSE OF WASHINGTON SQUARE! Alice singing and being a "big star" — and all those songs! But *oh* those ludicrous hats!

We liked LITTLE OLD NEW YORK too — wasn't our own Richard Greene with her? And didn't the 'ads' say "She fought the whole town to win him?" We were sorry she lost him — and her singing voice too — but we loved her in comedy.

HOLLYWOOD CAVALCADE was *the* crowning glory for us — our billboards merely said "Alice Faye in Technicolour!" Everyone went along to drool and sigh to find out her hair was so golden blonde and her eyes *so blue*! BARRICADE reached us in 1940 — all that China war — but *we* were at war too so we didn't want to see a non-singing Alice doing a Dietrich!

The name LILLIAN RUSSELL meant little to most of us — but who cared? Alice's name was bigger than the Russell one, and she was singing again — and being so glamorous — yet so sweet too!

Yes, we were at war. Everything was rationed — we had the complete blackout — but for a couple of hours for six pennies we could forget everything but Alice singing our cares away! We began to get lend lease from America and food parcels — so when Alice arrived in TIN PAN ALLEY we could sing "America, I Love You" with her. Betty Grable meant little to us then — she was pretty — could dance — but couldn't sing like our Alice so we had no qualms!

By 1941, clothes were rationed, just about everything — but movies — was. We hadn't seen real fruit for two years — it was grey, black and dreary, and the future looked worse. But along came THAT NIGHT IN RIO and all that colour. The box office returns went higher than the barrage balloons — or the spitfires. This was *IT*. Something we'd dreamed about. A world full of glamour, gorgeous scenery, beautiful women, fascinating music — and breathtaking gowns — the *LOT*. We had an orgy of indulgence in eye-filling splendour. We could have eaten Miranda's

hats — plastic or not. And there was Alice — in black, in blue, in gold, in pink — looking absolutely stunning. Audiences "oohed" and "aahed" at her every appearance!

Then, in GREAT AMERICAN BROADCAST with all the menfolk away fighting someone, somewhere — the women all went along to see Alice — and listen to her voice say exactly what they wanted to say to their absent loves in "Where You Are" and "Long Ago Last Night."

To the boys in the services Alice had become the epitome of the girls they'd left behind! They had Betty Grable pinned up on the barrack wall for glamour! And Dottie Lamour to remind them that *all* jungles and tropic islands weren't the hell holes they were in now! Lana Turner was there for sex, but Alice was the picture they kept in their breast pocket. She symbolised everything that was lovely, clean and wholesome and womanly — their wife, sweetheart, sister — the girl of a thousand dreams!

WEEK-END IN HAVANA proved an even greater hit than RIO had been! Even more colourful, brilliant and exotic. It did more for morale in Britain than Relief Aid could do. We found it gay and scintillating and it sure beat the blitz.

After that, no more films with Alice for a while. All we could do was anticipate her next one after she'd had her first baby. When the film did arrive — it was an even bigger sensation than HAVANA! HELLO, FRISCO, HELLO was a box office bonanza in London — and on its General Release throughout the country — everyone — but everyone flocked to it. We were really saying "Hello, Alice." There she was, looking more gorgeous, radiant — than ever before — really scrumptious in those period clothes — and singing song after song! "You'll Never Know" was the high spot in light music during our war years. It seemed to chrystalise all that everyone wanted to say to absent loved ones! The ads read "Try and see it with the one you love — and when Alice sings 'You'll Never Know' just close your eyes and hold hands!"

THE GIRLS HE LEFT BEHIND (U.S. title was THE GANG'S ALL HERE) was another tuneful, fruit-laden trifle! It presented strawberries and bananas — things we'd not seen for five long years. Alice again brought us to tears with "No Love — No Nothing." But she looked so lovely and gay for "The Polka Dot Polka."

Just after the war we had her FALLEN AN-GEL but the timing was all wrong. We'd just had five years of misery and drabness and didn't want to pay to see more. We allowed Alice her moments of drama — but hoped she'd get back to colour and music for us. But no! Alice packed up her career altogether. But for a while we were very lucky. Several factors explained this. The government intervention in the film industry. Making a sort of quota — whereby film companies were limited as to numbers of films they could bring into the country. Thus to give the British film industry a chance to develop. Shortage of raw film and material faced our industry. So the companies had to reissue the old films to keep the English markets open. Even though 20th Century-Fox had built up Grable, Haver, Blaine — we still had reissues of Faye films to show alongside the new girls. The comparisons were not kind to the new girls. They lacked Alice's warmth, sincerity and class. So in 1946-47 ON THE AVENUE could *still* hold its own with THE DOLLY SISTERS and DOLL FACE.

Even though Alice was not making films — the English were still loyal. Magazines and newspapers were always carrying letters demanding a comeback by Alice during the fifties. Other big stars of her era had faded. Some were "bigger" stars than she — in their dramatic or comedy films, but no one seemed to want comebacks by Norma Shearer, Janet Gaynor, Mae West or others.

20th Century-Fox in London had huge files of correspondence on Alice — either demanding come-backs, or reissues. Now and again they'd reissue an old movie just to keep us happy and quiet for a while. Yes, though new stars kept coming up — some to shine brightly — others to flicker and die — the English remained Faithful to Faye — she held a unique place in our hearts!

When she finally *did* emerge from her self-imposed seclusion for STATE FAIR the response was so great! Even Fox in London was amazed! Throughout the country Alice was the "draw" for FAIR. Pat Boone may have drawn the teenagers — but the older crowd flocked to see Alice! So great was the response that Fox capitalized on this and in January 1963 they revived ALEXANDER'S RAGTIME BAND at their Rialto cinema in London's West End — even launching it with a press showing too! All

the newspapers re-reviewed it — and all did so in glowing terms — praising its entertainment values — and above all, Alice. It ran for three weeks — and was well attended. No mean achievement for an old movie twenty-five years young.

It was the first Faye movie we had on TV in 1966. Fox was the last company to sell to TV here. Response was even greater — and other Faye films quickly followed. In fact BBC still states they get more requests to show Faye films than any other star's.

Very few in England had received her radio shows with Phil Harris. We never saw her do a TV show in England. Americans were lucky in that respect. So how come — that the English Love Affair with Alice Faye still continued?

Her visits to England were always private affairs — but in 1970 — we managed to contact her at her London hotel when she accompanied Phil for a TV show filmed here. She asked, "Why do you still remember me??" We couldn't really explain it! She was gracious enough to visit a London Cinema Club for a showing of two of her old films. Her fans were there in force to meet and cheer her. Alice was in tears — and could only murmer, "It's so wonderful to be remembered."

In 1971 *Liberty* magazine voted her "Film Star to Be Remembered" in New York. Again, the key word — remember! Why *do* we remember her?

What did she have that the other stars lacked — to be so fondly remembered? Was it that husky, haunting, velvet singing voice? Her blonde beauty? Her charm? Those blue-blue eyes — that always seemed to be on the brink of tears?

All of these and more — added to those attributes was her warmth, sincerity, complete lack of artifice — and that golden glow of the super-star. Anyone who was lucky enough to fall under the Faye spell could never forget to RE-MEMBER. The English certainly haven't forgotten Alice Faye. She is remembered with love, affection and she'll always hold a special place in our hearts!

Dear Alice — to misquote one of your songs — and with apologies to Irving Berlin — who I'm sure won't mind — "Remember, we said we love you true?

The English will not forget to remember!"

THE HARLOW STAR

1934·1936

Who could have foretold in the early months of 1934 that a shy, introverted blonde from a New York chorus line and a recent radio personality would become a depression star in her first film? It was indeed a story typical of the dime novel or at best a plot line from a Hollywood film. That it did happen just that way is no less strange in that Alice Faye herself had never dreamed of becoming a movie star in her first film, GEORGE WHITE'S SCANDALS. When Rudy Vallee returned East minus his vocalist it was a simple matter of sink or swim alone. Alice swam upstream alone, determined that she would succeed in a business she knew nothing about.

In a sense the Harlow image forced upon her was unfortunate, but the early Bette Davis had to face a period of blonde sex-pot apprenticeship which did little to further her career. Both stars, working in different fields, succeeded and reached the top rung of stardom and acclaim.

It is a credit to Faye's will to succeed in the movies, not to mention her obvious asset, that warm, deep voice which quickly caught on, that she was a star from the start of her career. In two years she starred in eight films, but not all of them were memorable. The promise in SCANDALS' wasn't entirely realized in NOW I'LL TELL, but the role of Peggy wasn't an easy one for a nineteen year old girl to make believable.

The good-natured, warm-hearted Faye gathered a following even in some rather indifferent pictures. She projected a quality of sincerity that often was an extension of her own casual charm, even when doubt and uncertainty dogged her footsteps.

Close examination of her next five films after NOW I'LL TELL shows a striking similarity in that the characters she played were essentially two dimensional. They were good-hearted gals eager to please and get ahead. Essentially that was what Alice was attempting in her career.

As Pat Doran in KING OF BURLESQUE she was given a well-written script, and she proved she could act as well as sing. If the makeup in this and her next, POOR LITTLE RICH GIRL, wasn't right, it proved that talent will tell. With a voice like that she couldn't lose, and the Harlow period had served to establish her in films though somewhat submerging her own natural charms under a false veneer of artificiality.

George White's Scandals

A Fox Picture 1934

With Cliff "Ukelele" Edwards on the set of GEORGE WHITE'S SCANDALS.

CAST:

Jimmy Martin	RUDY VALLEE
Happy McGillicuddy	JIMMY DURANTE
Kitty Donnelly	ALICE FAYE
Barbara Loraine	Adrienne Ames
Nicholas Mitwoch	Gregory Ratoff
Stew Hart	Cliff Edwards
Patsy Dey	Dixie Dunbar
Miss Lee	Gertrude Michael
Minister	Richard Carle
Pete Pandos	Warren Hymer
George White	Himself
Al Burke	Thomas Jackson
Count Dekker	Armand Kaliz
Sailor Brown	Roger Grey
Harold Bestry	William Bailey
John R. Loraine	George Irving
Judge O'Neill	Ed Le Saint
Eleanor Sawyer	Edna May Jones

CREDITS:

Directors	George White
	Thornton Freeland
	Harry Lachman
Story	George White
Additional dialogue	Jack Yellen
Photography	Lee Garmes, A.S.C.
	George Schneiderman, A.S.C.
Recording Engineers	A. L. Von Kirbach
	George Leverett
Editor	Paul Weatherwax
Wardrobe	Charles LeMaire
Dance Director	George Hale
Musical direction	Louis De Francesco

Released March 16, 1934. Running time 80 minutes.

SONGS: "Nasty Man," "So Nice," "Hold My Hand," "My Dog Loves Your Dog," "Sweet and Simple," "Six Women," "Following in Mother's Footsteps," "Every Day Is Father's Day with Baby," by Ray Henderson, Jack Yellen, and Irving Caesar. "Picking Cotton," by B. B. DeSylva, Lew Brown and Ray Henderson. "The Man on the Flying Trapeze" (traditional) Walter O'Keefe.

SYNOPSIS: Eager to obtain material for a Sunday news feature, Miss Lee gets George White's permission to watch a performance of his "Scandals" from backstage. Kitty, one of the show's featured stars, is obviously in love with Jimmy Martin, the name act of the show. However, Barbara Loraine, a society play-girl, has completely bewitched Jimmy. Kitty and Barbara quarrel in Jimmy's dressing room and Kitty slaps Barbara. Jimmy, who has seen the encounter from the doorway, sides with Barbara, and the disappointed Kitty plans to leave the show immediately. At the same time Happy, who fancies himself in love with Kitty, has a falling out with Patsy, and they too plan to quit the show. White meanwhile is badgered by Mitwoch, a salesman peddling everything from insurance to a bulletproof vest. During a radio broadcast of one of the show's numbers, a former prizefighter friend of Happy's shows up Barbara for just what she is, a celebrity-seeking hanger-on. White gets Kitty and Jimmy to sign a marriage license which each thinks is a contract for next season's show. In the finale number a judge is substituted for the minister, and Jimmy and Kitty are married assuring White of a successful run of his "Scandals."

NOTES AND REVIEWS: When White brought his "Scandals" idea to Fox for a screen musical, Vallee was to star with Lilian Harvey. After preliminary work began on the production, Miss Harvey demanded her role be expanded. When the studio refused, she left the cast and Fox quickly moved Alice Faye into her role. Originally Alice was to have one number and only featured billing. Her number, the first in the film, "Oh, You Nasty Man," proved to be so successful and her face and figure so well suited to the techniques of filming that her role and the Harvey role became one. A new star was born, and a studio campaign was begun to introduce Fox's new singing star. In addition to her opening production number she appeared in three others. Vallee sang "Hold My Hand" to her, she walked through "My Dog Loves Your Dog," with a pooch on a leash, and was part of "Sweet and Simple," an appealing flashback number in which she and Vallee were required to age convincingly. She and Vallee were then united in the finale wedding scene.

Despite the weakest of story threads on which to hang almost a dozen musical numbers, SCANDALS holds up remarkably well today due to impressive work on the part of a capable cast, some excellent music, cleverly staged musical numbers (dancing couples in the "Hold My Hand" number are reflected in a large garden pool while dozens of carefully groomed breeds of dogs parade endlessly through "My Dog Loves Your Dog"). In typical Hollywood fashion this "stage" production defied for size, scope, and setting any stage Broadway could possibly offer. The film shows expensive mounting, superb costume design in the gowns worn by the principals and chorines alike, and clever, if not always original, production numbers. "Every Day Is Father's Day with Baby" is a poor man's attempt at Busby Berkeley staging, but Alice's main number is a show stopper complete with unique miniature trick photography requiring a chorus girl to dive from the edge of a hand-held champagne glass into the bubbly. Early in the film Cliff Edwards and Dixie Dunbar shine in a simple setting of "So Nice."

"Platinum blonde Alice Faye is a distinct addition to the screen. Easy to look at and with a personality and voice, she puts over her numbers in great style," said Louella Parsons in her

With Rudy Vallee in the "Hold My Hand" production number.

With Jimmy Durante.

With Rudy Vallee in the "Sweet and Simple" production number.

syndicated column. Richard Watts Jr., writing in the *New York Herald Tribune* said: "If you see eye to eye with me about film revues you should enjoy Mr. Durante as he dons blackface and sings a combination of all the songs about going back to that dear old Southland, and be entertained by Miss Faye as she puts over the best song number of the photoplay in effective style, but will not feel exactly overrun with thoughts about the brotherhood of man while these baby chorus girls are performing." (Latter remark referred to the "Following in Mother's Footsteps" number.) Philip K. Scheuer, writing in the *N.Y. Times*, remarked, "The two best numbers are staged shortly after the first 'curtain.' I refer to the hot tune called "You Nasty Man" which

comes closest to the cinematic patterns evolved during the current cycle by Busby Berkeley, and to 'Hold My Hand,' which is much the most melodious of the songs and virtually the only one with grace. Alice Faye, a flashy blond newcomer, puts over the 'Nasty Man' lyrics in great style, while Rudy Vallee, returning after many months to croon sonorously in her ear, pleads to have his hand held." *Variety* added: "Of the cast members, Alice Faye probably will draw most of the comment. She is pretty much on the spot, having been widely publicized, and in an important part in her first picture. Faye girl, in looks and performance is a pleasant surprise, Of course, she sings adequately, for that's her business."

With Adrienne Ames.

With Rudy Vallee.

*With Rudy Vallee
in the "Sweet and Simple"
production number.*

30

With the White Scan-dolls in the "Nasty Man" production number.

With Rudy Vallee and chorus in the "Hold My Hand" production number.

Now I'll Tell

A Fox Picture 1934

CAST:

Murray Golden	SPENCER TRACY
Virginia Golden	Helen Twelvetrees
Peggy Warren	Alice Faye
Mositer	Robert Gleckler
Doran	Henry O'Neill
Freddie	Hobart Cavanaugh
Hart	G. P. Huntley, Jr.
Mary	Shirley Temple
Tommy Jr.	Ronnie Cosbey
Traylor	Ray Cooke
Curtis	Frank Marlowe
Wynne	Barbara Weeks
Joe Ready	Theodore Newton
Mac	Leon Ames

with

Vince Barnett, Clarence Wilson, and Jim Donlon

CREDITS:

Director	Edwin Burke
Producer	Winfield Sheehan
Screen play	Edwin Burke
Story	Mrs. Arnold Rothstein
Photography	Ernest Palmer, A.S.C.
Settings	Jack Otterson
Sound	William D. Flick
Gowns	Rita Kaufman
Musical director	Arthur Lange
Musical score	Hugh Friedhofer
	Arthur Lange
	David Buttolph

Released June 8, 1934. Running time 87 minutes.

SONGS: "Foolin' with the Other Woman's Man" and "Harlem Versus the Jungle" by Lew Brown and Harry Akst.

SYNOPSIS: Murray Golden is a young man in a hurry to make his pile. He will gamble on anything, and due to his glib manner, self-confidence, and drive to succeed he becomes a well-heeled gambler. His wife, Virginia, sees less and less of him, and her life is merely an empty void. His position prevents her from belonging or being accepted by the people she longs to be part of. Murray promises he will quit when he makes $500,000, but he goes back on his word as the money rolls in. Murray meets Peggy, a young, vivacious singer. They fall in love, and she becomes his mistress. Turning a deaf ear to her pleas of marriage, Murray wants his life to continue as it is with a wife he idolizes at home and Peggy for the heedless whirl of activity he cannot do without. Mositer, out to get Murray for a fixed fight which lost him a fortune, kidnaps Virginia. Speeding back to New York Murray is injured in a car crash, and Peggy is killed.

A FOX FILM

SPENCER TRACY

in

NOW I'LL TELL

with

HELEN TWELVETREES

ALICE FAYE

ROBERT GLECKLER   HOBART CAVANAUGH

HENRY O'NEILL   SHIRLEY TEMPLE

Direction & Screenplay by Edwin Burke

From a story by Mrs. Arnold Rothstein

Music & Lyrics by LEW BROWN & HARRY AKST

1934

With Hobart Cavanaugh on the set of NOW I'LL TELL.

With Spencer Tracy.

Virginia, unable to stand an intolerable situation, leaves Murray and sails for Europe and a divorce. Again and again Murray runs against Mositer, and his luck is gone now that Virginia has left him. Realizing his time is running out, Murray, using his wife's jewels, purchases a big insurance policy. Refusing to pay his gambling losses Murray insults Mositer and is shot. Virginia reaches his bedside before he dies and promises him that he'll recover and that she will return to him so that things can be as they once were.

NOTES AND REVIEWS: Alice's second film was a prestige film in that she was costarred with Spencer Tracy, a bright young man who had been attracting a great deal of attention. He would make only three more films for Fox and then move to M-G-M to become one of the all-time movie greats. Alice, as the other woman, had the smallest part of her entire career, but due to Burke's skillful direction in a well-written part it was a step up and better than her next three films in which she starred.

Faye's one musical number, "Foolin' with the Other Woman's Man" was a number which has to be seen to be believed. She was dressed all in black satin, overly adorned with dark feathers, and carried a huge black feathered fan. Her hair was a frizzled mass of white curls, and the makeup was dark and heavy. The effect was starkly hard and the most extreme of her entire career. *Variety* said, "Alice Faye looking rather buxom, shines as the other woman." It was to be the only film in which Alice died in the course of the story's unreeling.

For the record the official title was NOW I'LL TELL BY MRS. ARNOLD ROTHSTEIN. It was seldom used as too long for most theatre marquees. Most of the advertising utilized the first three words only. In England the title was changed to WHILE NEW YORK SLEEPS, but whatever the title Mrs. Rothstein had written the original story about her gambler husband and Fox merely changed the names.

One name in the cast would, within a few months, become the famed mortgage raiser at Fox. Shirley Temple had a tiny bit of only four lines as the daughter of Henry O'Neill. It was one of four bit parts (often just walk-ons) which Shirley did in 1934, but NOW I'LL TELL reached the screen after STAND UP AND CHEER, by which time her name would be a national institution. Faye would appear twice more in Temple films within the next two years.

The Arnold Rothstein story in a somewhat different treatment had already provided the plot for "Street of Chance," a widely acclaimed 1930 Paramount film in which William Powell and Kay Francis appear in the husband and wife roles and the part played by Alice was omitted.

With Clarence Hummel Wilson, G.P. Huntley Jr., Spencer Tracy, Robert Gleckler, Eddie Kane and Hobart Cavanaugh.

FOOLIN' WITH THE OTHER WOMAN'S MAN

Words and Music by

LEW BROWN
and
HARRY AKST

As sung by
ALICE FAYE
in the Fox picture

Now I'll Tell
by Mrs. Arnold Rothstein

with

SPENCER TRACY
HELEN TWELVETREES

With Hobart Cavanaugh.

35

She Learned About Sailors

A Fox Production 1934

CAST:

Larry Wilson	LEW AYRES
Jean Legoi	ALICE FAYE
Jose Pedro Alesandro Lopez Rubinstein	Harry Green
Peanuts	Frank Mitchell
Eddie	Jack Durant
Brunette	Wilma Cox
Hotel Clerk	Paul McVey
Girl at Dance Hall	June Vlasek (June Lang)

with:

Ray McClennan, Pete Rasch, Ed Lee, Allen Jung, Ernie Alexander, Russ Clark, Gay Seabrook, James Conlin, Edward LeSaint, Al Hill, Susan Fleming, and Harry Tung.

CREDITS:

Director	George Marshall
Producer	John Stone
Screen Play	William Counselman Henry Johnson
Story	Randall H. Faye
Photography	Harry Jackson
Sound	Bernard Freericks
Settings	Duncan Cramer
Gowns	Royer
Musical direction	Samuel Kaylin

Released June 29, 1934. Running time 76 minutes.

SONG: "Here's the Key to My Heart" by Richard Whiting and Sidney Clare.

SYNOPSIS: Larry, a sailor on liberty in Shanghai, meets Jean in a sleazy waterfront cafe, where she is currently singing. In short order their friendship turns to love, but Larry's ship departs for the states, and Jean is left alone. Fearing that his modest gob's pay isn't enough for them to live on, Larry writes Jean that they must not see each other again. His letter, however, is intercepted by his buddies Peanuts and Eddie. They substitute another in its place in which Larry declares his love. Jean embarks for Los Angeles and is waiting when the sailors steam into port. Complications follow in which Larry at first refuses to see or talk to Jean. Peanuts and Eddie add further fuel to the romantic blaze in their typical knockabout attempts to set Cupid on the proper road to romance. Flitting in and out of the madcap confusion is the persistent Jose Rubinstein, a South American impressario, with both a romantic and business eye on Jean. True love ultimately conquers all, and Larry and Jean end up in each other's arms at the final fadeout.

With Lew Ayres.

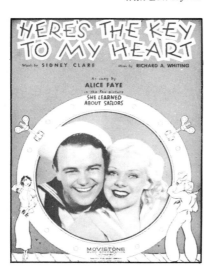

NOTES AND REVIEWS: In her third film, SHE LEARNED ABOUT SAILORS, Alice Faye was elevated to full-star status, playing the romantic lead and doing as well as a weak screenplay and tight-fisted economy would allow. It was her first of three co-starring stints with the wildly physical comedians, Mitchell and Durant. It seems incredible that thirty-five years ago critics and public alike found the team acceptable not to mention hilarious and that so much of this film's footage was reserved for their negligible talent.

The New York Times had reservations about the film in general and Faye in particular. ". . . it must regretfully be observed that Miss Faye, a promising Jean Harlow type with a sulphurous voice and personality, is not altogether happy in the role of the innocent maiden." *Film Weekly's* comment was brief, "Alice Faye is quite effective."

"Here's the Key to My Heart" was Faye's only song, but in the run-down cafe setting it was interestingly showcased. Certain Faye mannerisms were already becoming established in her vocal numbers, i.e., the quivering lower lip, sly wink, and redolent, lazy gait with the body weight supported on one leg and the other bent at the knee.

In typical Fox fashion of remaking properties already owned, this story would be reworked with few changes and reach the screen again in 1940 under the title SAILOR'S LADY with Jon Hall and Nancy Kelly in the leads. It created no great stir, and is notable only as providing a young film actor with his third small screen role. He would be Faye's costar five years later; his name — Dana Andrews.

With Harry Green.

Singing "Here's the Key to My Heart".

With Jack Durant, Frank Mitchell and Harry Green.

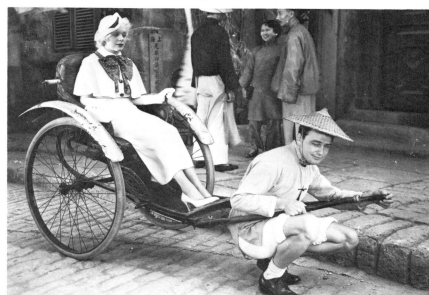

With Lew Ayres.

39

365 Nights in Hollywood

A Fox Picture 1934

CAST:

Jimmy Dale .... JAMES DUNN
Alice Perkins .... ALICE FAYE
Percy .... Frank Mitchell
Clarence .... Jack Durant
Professor Ellenbogen .... John Qualen
Adrian Almont .... John Bradford
Frank Young .... Frank Melton
J. Walter Delmar .... Grant Mitchell
Assistant Director .... Ray Cooke
Assistant D.A. .... Addison Richards
Drunk .... Arthur Housman
with:
Tyler Brooke, Paul McVey, Dick Whiting, Ben Hall, James Conlin, Frank Sully and Al Klein.

CREDITS:

Directed by .... George Marshall
Produced by .... Sol Wurtzel
Screenplay .... William Conselman
                                    Henry Johnson
Author .... Jimmy Starr
Photographed by .... Harry Jackson
Dances .... Sammy Lee
Music .... Richard Whiting

Released October 12, 1934. Running time 74 minutes.

SONGS: "My Future Star," and "Yes to You" by Sidney Clare and Richard Whiting.

SYNOPSIS: On a quiet Hollywood side street is the Delmar school of acting founded to train young hopefuls for screen careers. Its founder, J. Walter Delmar, is only interested in the tuition fees. He uses Adrian Almont, a former screen actor down on his luck, as bait to lure in student hopefuls. Alice comes to the school accompanied by Percy and Clarence, bumbling icemen, hoping for less chilly careers.

When Frank Young arrives with money to invest, Delmar suggests a film venture to star Alice. He even hires Jimmy, a has-been movie director given to drink, to handle the directing chores. Delmar's built-in escape clause is that should the production be halted for any reason, the money will be his by default.

Production begins, and Jimmy, realizing this is his only chance for a comeback, drives his crew without letup. The results are gratifying for all except Delmar. He induces Almont to take Alice away. Following a night of heavy drinking Almont passes out in his remote mountain cabin, and Alice is stranded with no way to get back to town.

Jimmy is frantic for his future in films as production grinds to a halt, and worried about Alice whom he now loves. At the last moment Percy and Clarence, back on the job as icemen, rescue Alice and return her to the studio where work resumes on the big production number finale. Delmar and Almont are apprehended, the film is a success, Frank's fortune is saved, and the careers and personal lives of Alice and Jimmy are assured.

With John Bradford and chorus for the "Yes, to You" production number.

With John Bradford.

With James Dunn and chorus for the finale production number "My Future Star."

NOTES AND REVIEWS: 365 NIGHTS IN HOLLYWOOD was the second film in a row that Alice made at the old Fox studio on Sunset Boulevard in Hollywood. For the remainder of her career her films would all be shot on the newer, more spacious lot near Beverly Hills. Again the script was a weak item from which director George Marshall exacted the full measure of potential.

The two musical numbers were full-scale production items of rather long duration. "Yes to You" was the more elaborate of the two. It started with Alice and twelve chorus boys in an ultra-modern ballroom setting. Dressed in a black sequined evening gown and waving another ostrich fan, this one white, it progressed to a huge, revolving globe of the world. In the dreamlike situation John Bradford pursued her with various stopovers in which Alice was dressed in the traditional costumes of diverse nationalities. "My Future Star" was the finale number in which Dunn had trouble making up his mind in which mold Alice would be best suited — Lupe Velez, Mae West, or Jean Harlow. Though clever and original it didn't quite come off and was merely busy.

Mitchell and Durant clowned their way through the proceedings for the second time in a Faye film, but mercifully had less footage than in SHE LEARNED ABOUT SAILORS or MUSIC IS MAGIC.

With only three films behind her, Alice was attracting attention and good notices. "Alice Faye as Alice Perkins, a girl who thinks she has talent, plays the part quite well," said *Film Weekly*, and *Picturegoer* seconded with, "Alice Faye scores heavily as the blonde girl who craves a chance in the movies."

Variety thought the acting capable and somewhat better than the material which inspired it. "James Dunn makes quite a little out of the thin part of the down-and-out who has fallen so low as to become a director in the fake school, but Grant Mitchell scoops with a suave performance as the school head. Miss Faye is pretty and fairly competent as the girl. John Bradford is the heavy, but the part is just a walk-through."

The concept of a film within a film was not a new idea. Faye did two more such productions: MUSIC IS MAGIC and HOLLYWOOD CAVALCADE, both superior to this early effort. Other stars and studios would further embellish the theme, most notably in: A STAR IS BORN, THE BAD AND THE BEAUTIFUL, THE STAR, THE BIG KNIFE, and the best of them all — SINGIN' IN THE RAIN.

With James Dunn, Frank Melton, and Dick Whiting.

With James Dunn.

With Frank Melton.

With Grant Mitchell and James Dunn.

43

George White's 1935 Scandals

A Fox Picture 1935

CAST:

Honey Walters .... ALICE FAYE
Eddie Taylor .... JAMES DUNN
Elmer White .... Ned Sparks
Manya .... Lyda Roberti
Dude Holloway .... Cliff Edwards
Midgie .... Arline Judge
Marilyn Collins .... Eleanor Powell
Aunt Jane .... Emma Dunn
Louis Pincus .... Benny Rubin
Harriman .... Charles Richman
Officer Riley .... Roger Imhof
Grady .... Donald Kerr
Daniels .... Walter Johnson
Master of ceremonies .... Fred Santley
Ticket seller .... Jack Mulhall
Porter .... Sam McDaniel
with

GEORGE WHITE

and:

Harry Dunkinson, Esther Brodelet, Fuzzy Knight, Thomas Jackson, Jed Prouty, Iris Shunn, and Lois Eckhart

CREDITS:

Entire Production Conceived, Produced and Directed by
George White
Screen play by .... Jack Yellen
                                    Patterson McNutt
Photography .... George Schneiderman, A.S.C.
Sound .... A. L. Von Kirbach
Dance ensembles by .... George White
Art director .... Gordon Wiles
Costumes .... Charles Le Maire
Musical direction .... Louis de Francesco

Released March 29, 1935. Running time 83 minutes.

SONGS: "According to the Moonlight" and "Oh, I didn't Know" by Jack Yellen, Herb Magidson and Joseph Meyer. "It's an Old Southern Custom," "I Was Born Too Late" by Jack Yellen and Joseph Meyer. "I Got Shoes, You Got Shosies," and "Hunkadola" by Jack Yellen, Cliff Friend and Joseph Meyer. "It's Time to Say Goodnight" by Cliff Friend and Joseph Meyer and "You Belong to Me" by Jack Yellen and Cliff Friend.

SYNOPSIS: Following the closing performance of his latest Scandals George White and Manya depart for a vacation in the Florida

In the "I Was Born Too Late" number.

sun. In a small Georgia town they come upon a theatre advertising "White's Scandals." The show is merely homegrown corn run by frozen-faced Elmer White, but one act offers possibilities. White offers singer Honey Walters a chance with his next Scandals. Fast-talking Aunt Jane gets George to take Eddie along too, and before he can escape, White is saddled with Elmer and bird-brained Midgie, and Manya adopts Dude.

Back in New York the latest Scandals opens to packed houses and critical acclaim, but complications arise when Eddie meets Marilyn Collins, a fast-stepping dancer with a powerful thirst. They become an item about town. Honey begins to step out as well. Her work suffers, she is frequently late, and finally both she and Eddie are out of the show.

Aunt Jane, worried because she has not heard from her niece, goes to New York. White sees her, rushes her into the theatre and puts out a desperate call for his two former stars. With the aid of booking agent Louis Pincus, Honey and Eddie return to the Scandals, and realizing the folly of their ways delight Aunt Jane with the news that they will marry.

With James Dunn for the "According to the Moonlight" number.

NOTES AND REVIEWS: After filming her previous two films at the smaller Fox lot in Hollywood, Alice returned to the main studio and received top billing for the first time in this latest edition of GEORGE WHITE'S SCANDALS. Her makeup and hair styles were an obvious attempt to cash in on the prevailing Harlow look, then much in vogue. With her hair bleached almost white, and her eyebrows plucked and penciled, her own personality was submerged in an image foreign and unfamiliar to her natural assets of warm, easygoing charm.

The depression was being felt throughout Hollywood. The weekly attendance in theatres throughout the nation had dropped alarmingly, and drastic cutbacks and economy measures were being employed to cut production costs. The 1935 SCANDALS felt the pinch, and while some clever photography by George Schneiderman was employed in the musical sequences, and several of the songs were given elaborate mounting, the results were heavy-handed. The production suffered from "too much plot" for a musical review as one critic noted.

Faye was given her most musical assignment to date. Her biggest number was the flashy, "Oh, I Didn't Know" with rows of chorus girls on different levels behind her. The number was quite similar to her "Nasty Man" number in the previous SCANDALS. The dancing chorines were ludicrous in that each seemed intent on doing her own thing; no one was together. Alice and Dunn did "According to the Moonlight" perched atop a stage moon for some nice moments, shared the "Hunkadola" with Edwards and Roberti for some acrobatic turns in which dummies were substituted for real dancers thereby removing what punch the number might otherwise have possessed. Alice was also heard in "You Belong to Me" and "It's an Old Southern Custom," latter number was repeated so often in the running time it became tiresome. One reviewer, Mae Tinee by name, wrote, "Miss Faye lusciously fulfills the double requirements of heroine and singing star. The key song, "It's an Old Southern Custom,' was, I thought, rather run to death."

Movie Mirror's Jerry Halliday seemed overly sold on Faye by enthusing, "Keep your eye on

With George White, Ned Sparks, James Dunn and Emma Dunn.

With the Scan-dolls for the "Oh, I Didn't Know" production number.

Alice Faye, Fox Films' new glamour gal. She has what it takes to hit the cinema heights. Alice plays her grandest role in this picture. And what a marvelous singin'-steppin' duo she and Jimmy Dunn make!"

Howard Barnes in his *New York Times* review agreed on Alice's assets, but he dismissed the film. "Alice Faye is the premiere chanteuse of the musical and is exceedingly resourceful in putting over its most infectious songs. Jack Yellen, Cliff Friend, and Joseph Meyer have coined some bright and catchy songs for the occasion and Charles Le Maire has dressed the show sumptuously, but neither the tunes nor pageantry are potent enough to charm away its frequent laggard stretches."

Eleanor Powell, making her screen debut here, came in for most of the cheers. She was destined to change the pattern of screen dancing entirely, and would, in a few short months, become the movies' most prominent dancer. For some strange reason Fox did not sign her to a long-term contract. She was quickly snapped up by M-G-M where she reigned supreme in some highly original and skillfully photographed musicals for the next eight years.

Every Night at Eight

A Paramount Picture 1935

CAST:

Tops Cardona	**GEORGE RAFT**
Dixie Dean	**ALICE FAYE**
Daphne O'Connor	Patsy Kelly
Susan Moore	Frances Langford
Three Radio Rogues	Jimmie Hollywood
	Henry Taylor
	Eddie Bartel
Snorky	Harry Barris
Master of Ceremonies	Walter Catlett
Trick Drummer	Dillon Ober
Henrietta (Chicken Lady)	Florence Gill

with:
Herman Bing, Charles Forsyth, Booth Howard, John H. Dilson, and Bud Flanagan (Dennis O'Keefe).

CREDITS:

Director	Raoul Walsh
Producer	Walter Wanger
Screen play	Gene Towne
	Graham Baker
Additional dialogue	Bert Hanlon
From the original story	
"Three on a Mike" by	Stanley Garvey
Photography	James Van Trees
Art direction	Alexander Toluboff
Musical setting	S. K. Wineland
Sound	Hugh Grenzbach
Wardrobe designed & executed by	Helen Taylor
Film editor	W. Donn Hayes
Assistant director	Eric Stacey

Released August 2, 1935. Running time 80 minutes

SONGS: "Take It Easy," "Speaking Confidentially," "I'm in the Mood for Love," "Every Night at Eight," by Jimmy McHugh and Dorothy Fields, and "I Feel a Song Comin' On" by Jimmy McHugh, Dorothy Fields and George Oppenheimer. "Then You've Never Been Blue," Music by Ted Fio Rito, Lyrics by Joe Young, Sam Lewis, and Francis Langford.

SYNOPSIS: Dixie, Daphne, and Susan, office workers at Huxley's Mint Julep Company, have just made a hit at the employees' variety show. Spurred on by their success and eager to hear themselves they are caught making a record on the boss's dictaphone and fired.

Locked out of their rooming house for non-payment of rent they seemingly have hit bottom until a passing truck advertising an amateur radio show makes them contestants. They are almost a hit until Susan, weak from hunger, faints during their number, and top money goes to Tops Cardona and his band. Tops takes pity on the girls, treats them to a meal, and after

With Patsy Kelly.

With Frances Langford and Patsy Kelly.

Singing "I Feel a Song Comin' On."

With George Raft, Patsy Kelly and Frances Langford.

With Frances Langford and Patsy Kelly.

hearing Susan plaintively sing a number asks the trio to team up with him in a bid for the bigtime. But the bigtime is a long time in coming, though they all click in a cabaret-restaurant.

Finally the break comes, and from three offers they eagerly sign to star nightly on a radio hookup for Huxley's Mint Julep Company. Now it is fancy gowns, jewels, fur coats and fame, but Tops keeps the girls so busy they have no time for socializing. Fed up with his manner of running their lives, though it is obvious Tops and Susan are in love, the three girls accept a weekend invitation to a society yachting party. The snooty uppercrusters are too rich for the girls' blood, and at the last moment they hurry back to the broadcasting studio where Tops is flops without his songbirds. At the fadeout Susan is in Tops' arms and everyone (?) is happy.

NOTES AND REVIEWS: EVERY NIGHT AT EIGHT remains a curious film item in that it is the first of but two picture assignments Faye was cast in outside her home studio of Fox. In it she received second billing under Raft, then a big name at Paramount, but Frances Langford, here essaying her film debut was the romantic interest — not Faye. As *Variety* noted, "Oddly, the casting has the stars actually supporting Frances Langford, newcomer from radio, with Alice Faye taking the worst of the drubbing." The music is topnotch right down the line with "I Feel a Song Comin' On" the big production number halfway through the proceedings done very Mae Westian in delivery with Alice resembling Jean Harlow more obviously than in any other film. The behind-the-scenes peek at radio broadcasting was excellent, especially the amateur hour presided over by Walter Catlett, a thinly-disguised Major Bowes, then much in vogue. *Photoplay* for October 1935 enthused: "... it's a photographed radio program — but there's plenty to entertain you, meaning George Raft in a likable role, Alice Faye, Frances Langford, Patsy Kelly and many haunting new tunes." Of particular interest were the costumes of Helen Taylor, an elaborate parade of sequins, velveted bodices, yards of tulle, lace, and some of the most outlandish furs seen this side of Orry-Kelly. Ironic too that for a change Patsy Kelly, usually a ragpicker gone wrong, appeared in lovely clothes and handled the assignment with aplomb and self assurance.

With Frances Langford, George Raft and Patsy Kelly.

Music Is Magic

A Fox Film (20th Century-Fox) 1935

End of the "La Locumba" number
with Jack Durant and Frank Mitchell.

CAST:

Peggy Harper .... ALICE FAYE
Jack Lambert .... Ray Walker
Diane DeValle .... Bebe Daniels
Peanuts Harper .... Frank Mitchell
Eddie Harper .... Jack Durant
Shirley DeValle .... Rosina Lawrence
Tony Bennett .... Thomas Beck
Pomeroy .... Andrew Tombes
Castellano .... Luis Alberni
Amanda .... Hattie McDaniel
Jim Waters .... Hal K. Dawson
Theatre Manager .... Charles C. Wilson
Theatre Cashier .... Lynn Bari

CREDITS:

Director .... George Marshall
Associate Producer .... John Stone
Screenplay .... Edward Eliscu and Lou Breslow
From a play by Gladys Unger and Jesse Lasky, Jr.
Photography .... L. W. O'Connell, A.S.C.
Sound .... Bernard Freericks
Editor .... Alexander Troffey
Art director .... Duncan Cramer
Dance director .... Jack Donohue
Gowns .... Rega
Musical director .... Samuel Kaylin

Released November 1, 1935. Running time 66 minutes.

SONGS: "Honey Chile" and "Love Is Smiling at Me" by Oscar Levant and Sidney Clare. "Music Is Magic" by Arthur Johnston and Sidney Clare. "La Locumba" by Raul Roulien and Sidney Clare.

With Ray Walker, Thomas Beck, Bebe Daniels,
Jack Durant, and Frank Mitchell.

SYNOPSIS: On a personal appearance tour, Diane DeValle is faced with the fact that she is no longer a box-office draw. Audiences are small and lukewarm to her singing though enthusiastic about the talents of young Peggy Harper, part of a comedy, singing act. When the tour is cancelled Peggy joins her partners, the Harpers, and Jack Lambert to try their luck in Hollywood. But the film capital proves a tough nut to crack and Peggy ends up working in a laundry. Even a scheme to sing for Mr. Pomeroy, a studio official dining in a Mexican

With Ray Walker.

restaurant, fails, though the Harper brothers wreck the place with a Tarzan act. Meanwhile Diane returns to Hollywood to resume her picture career. With her she brings Shirley DeValle, her daughter that she has, until now, successfully passed off as her younger sister. Piqued when Tony Bennett turns from her to Shirley, Diane squelches the romance. Rehearsals start on "Music Is Magic," Diane's new film in which Peggy has a job in the chorus line. When Diane refuses to follow directions for a song and "get hot," Jack, pretending he is Pomeroy's representative, asks Peggy to sing the song. She clicks and everyone is pleased but Diane. When Shirley is slightly injured while leaving the dressing room of her mother, Diane, realizing her mistake, openly recognizes the girl, gets Pomeroy to give Peggy the role in "Music Is Magic" and agrees to accept a mother role the studio has for her, if it "Can be a kind of a young mother." Peggy, Jack, and the Harpers become a sensation in the film.

NOTES AND REVIEWS: MUSIC IS MAGIC began life with the title BALL OF FIRE, a meaningless moniker quickly dropped. It was inadvertently the Faye film known for its firsts and lasts. It was the first Faye film to bear the new 20th Century-Fox trademark; the first film of actor Ray Walker, and the last U.S. screen appearance of Bebe Daniels. It was also Alice's last screen teaming with Mitchell and Durant, a comedy team which, viewed today, seems entirely lacking in humor and very old hat.

It should be remembered that the old Fox company, who produced this film, was then on its last legs and in the process of merging with 20th Century, so expenses were cut to the bone. Musical numbers, except for the finale title tune, were brief and indifferently staged to say nothing of stock costumes and second-time-around sets. Still, the story was alive, and the performers under Marshall's direction overcame its obvious shortcomings. Editing was brisk; the running time of sixty-six minutes was the shortest of any Faye film.

Alice was given top billing, but it was Daniels' film from start to finish. As *Photoplay* stated: "Bebe Daniels steps out and shows 'em some real trouping in this pleasant little semi-musical,

With Ray Walker, Hal K. Dawson, Luis Alberni, and Andrew Tombes.

With Ray Walker.

With Frank Mitchell, Ed Gargan, Jack Durant, and Ray Walker.

With Frank Mitchell, Jack Durant, and Ray Walker.

headed by Alice Faye and Ray Walker, of the vaudeville gal who finally makes the grade in Hollywood."

To illustrate the lack of attention to detail, Hattie McDaniel's role was listed in the end credits as "Amanda," but she was always referred to as "Hattie" throughout the film.

Alice's best number, "Honey Chile," was never completely sung, having dialogue and comedy routines breaking it up. At best MUSIC IS MAGIC is one of those pleasant little films

which deserved more, but usually ended up the second half of a double bill. *Variety* warned, "Despite some rare comic moments by Mitchell and Durant, neat work by Alice Faye, and nice contribution by Bebe Daniels, 'Music Is Magic' is one of those flighty affairs that will have to struggle getting past the dual barricade."

The last word of that review was strangely prophetic; four years later the Faye film most authorities considered her most unfortunate would bear that title — BARRICADE.

King of Burlesque

A 20th Century-Fox Picture 1936
A Darryl F. Zanuck Production

CAST:

Kerry Bolton	WARNER BAXTER
Pat Doran	ALICE FAYE
Joe Cooney	JACK OAKIE
Connie	Arline Judge
Rosalind Cleve	Mona Barrie
Kolpolpeck	Gregory Ratoff
Marie	Dixie Dunbar
Ben	Fats Waller
Anthony Lamb	Nick Long, Jr.
Arthur	Kenny Baker
Stanley Drake	Charles Quigley
Wong	Keye Luke
The Bootblack	Gareth Joplin

with
Andrew Tombes, Shirley Deane, Harry (Zoop) Welch, Claudie Coleman, Ellen E. Lowe, Herbert Ashley, Jerry Mandy, the Paxton Sisters and Shaw and Lee.

CREDITS:

Director	Sidney Lanfield.
Associate Producer	Kenneth MacGowan.
Screenplay	Gene Markey .Harry Tugend

Adaptation by James Seymour, based on the story by Vina Delmar.

Dance ensembles	Sammy Lee
Music and lyrics	Jimmy McHugh, Ted Koehler, Jack Yellen and Lew Pollack
Photography	Peverell Marley, A.S.C.
Art direction	Hans Peter
Settings	Thomas Little
Assistant director	A. F. Erickson
Film editor	Ralph Dietrich
Costumes	Gwen Wakeling
Sound	E. Clayton Ward Roger Heman
Musical direction	Victor Baravalle.

Released January 3, 1936. Running time 88 minutes.

SONGS: "I'm Shooting High," "I've Got My Fingers Crossed," "Spreading Rhythm Around," "Whose Big Baby Are You?" "Lovely Lady" by Jimmy McHugh and Ted Koehler. "I Love to Ride the Horses on a Merry-go-round" by Jack Yellen and Lew Pollack.

SYNOPSIS: Kerry Bolton, New York's most successful entrepreneur of the G-string runway, decides to go into legit musical production as burlesque lacks "class." Pat, his choreographer and first string singer, along with Joe, Bolton's right-hand man, doubt the wisdom of the move. Kerry's string of hit musicals soon proves that he knows his business. Hard-working Pat, wearing her heart on her sleeve for Kerry, is unable to make him see that she is more than just a good hoofer. Kerry takes Pat, Joe, and Connie with him to the Park Avenue auction of the furnishings belonging to once-wealthy Rosalind Cleve. He makes a bad impression on Rosalind and she refuses to sell him a ship model. Later needing money desperately, Rosalind comes to Kerry's office to sell the model. The deal doesn't go through, but Bolton is impressed with the poise, bearing, and breeding of the society woman. Following a whirlwind courtship they marry. Pat, heartsick and discouraged, goes to London where her singing makes her the toast of the town. Rosalind now exerts a strong influence over Kerry, and when they return to New York following a European honeymoon, she asks him to star her former protegee, Stanley Drake, in a new show.

With Gregory Ratoff and Jack Oakie.

With Charles Quigley, Mona Barrie, Warner Baxter,
Arline Judge and Jack Oakie.

With Warner Baxter and Kenny Baker.

Putting aside the know-how which brought him to the top, Bolton tries to stage the perfect show with class and sophistication. The cost is staggering, and when it finally opens the show lacks the Bolton touch and is a financial disaster. Bolton, now broke, is quickly divorced by Rosalind and is to be found more frequently drinking himself into a stupor in second-rate bars. Pat returns to New York and she and Joe hire Kolpolpeck to impersonate a millionaire eager to back Bolton in a show biz comeback. The ruse works and Kerry opens a new type theatre-restaurant. Pat does the dances as before and agrees to star, while Kerry casts Ben, the elevator man; a dancing bootblack; Marie, a telephone operator with a yen to dance; Arthur, a former office boy who sings; and Lamb, a Hollywood dancer. The show is a smash hit, Kerry is once more on top, the money is rolling in, and he and Pat are reunited as are Joe and the always available Connie.

NOTES AND REVIEWS: In her eighth film, Alice Faye came into her own as a full-fledged star. This was to be the turning point in her career — no more second rate stories indifferently produced. Darryl F. Zanuck, realizing the potential of her growing box office draw began grooming her for better things. Her makeup and hairstyles were still too Harlow-influenced, but her rendition of "Whose Big Baby Are You?" "Shooting High," and "I Love to Ride the Horses" showed great promise of what was soon to become a major musical talent. *Variety* stated: "Miss Faye sings satisfactorily and looks well despite a too-fluffy coiffure. Her best is a novelty song skit in which Herbert Mundin plays straight."

KING OF BURLESQUE was actually similar to Warner Brothers' FOOTLIGHT PARADE in that most of the musical numbers came at the end when Baxter's new venture bore fruit. Baxter was merely going through the routines of another 42ND STREET role, and was destined to costar in one more Faye film taking second billing to Alice in BARRICADE. The entire production of BURLESQUE was almost identical to 1943's HELLO, FRISCO, HELLO in which John Payne gave more assurance to the producer role and Alice and Jack Oakie enacted their original roles a second time.

With Nick Long Jr. and chorus from the production number "I'm Shooting High."

th Warner Baxter.

With Vernon Downing.

With Jack Oakie.

Poor Little Rich Girl

A 20th Century-Fox Picture 1936
Darryl F. Zanuck In Charge of Production

CAST:

Barbara Barry	SHIRLEY TEMPLE
Jerry Dolan	ALICE FAYE
Margaret Allen	Gloria Stuart
Jimmy Dolan	Jack Haley
Richard Barry	Michael Whalen
Collins	Sara Haden
Woodward	Jane Darwell
Simon Peck	Claude Gillingwater
George Hathaway	Paul Stanton
Tony	Henry Armetta
Stebbins	Charles Coleman
Percival Gooch	Arthur Hoyt
Flagin	John Wray
Dan Ward	Tyler Brooke
Tony's wife	Mathilde Comont
Radio vocalist	Tony Martin

CREDITS:

Director	Irving Cummings
Associate Producer	B. G. DeSylva
Screenplay	Sam Hellman, Gladys Lehman and Harry Tugend
Suggested by the stories of Eleanor Gates and Ralph Spence.	
Music and lyrics	Mack Gordon and Harry Revel
Dances	Jack Haskell, Ralph Cooper
Photography	John Seitz, A.S.C.
Art direction	William Darling
Associate	Rudolph Sternad
Settings	Thomas Little
Assistant director	Booth McCracken
Film Editor	Jack Murray
Costumes	Gwen Wakeling
Sound	S. C. Chapman, Roger Heman
Musical direction	Louis Silvers
Musical adaptation	Cyril J. Mockridge

Released July 24, 1936. Running time 72 minutes.

SONGS: "Oh, My Goodness!" "Buy a Bar of Barry's," "When I'm With You," "But Definitely," "You Gotta Eat Your Spinach, Baby," and "Military Man" by Mack Gordon and Harry Revel.

SYNOPSIS: Motherless Barbara Barry has everything a child could want: a wealthy soap manufacturer for a father, toys, clothes, and pets, to say nothing of a private nurse. Collins rushes her charge into bed at the first sneeze, but it is Woodward who suggests that Mr. Barry send his daughter to school so that she can be with other children.

It is decided that Collins will take Barbara away to school, but outside the railroad station the nurse is struck by a car, rushed to the hospital, and Barbara decides to become Betsy Ware, the heroine in her favorite book that Woodward, the housekeeper, reads to her.

She meets Tony and his monkey and follows them home for the night insisting she is an orphan. The following morning hearing dance steps from the flat above, Barbara imitates the steps so perfectly that Jimmy and his wife Jerry hurry down to see who the "smart hoofer" really is.

The two ex-vaudeville performers casually adopt "Betsy," work up an act — Dolan, Dolan and Dolan — and proceed to sell it on radio. Simon Peck, an irascible rival soap manufacturer, buys the act after Barbara wanders into his office and inadvertently softens him up.

Barbara's father, meanwhile, has fallen in love with Peck's secretary, Margaret, and while visiting her one evening hears his daughter, now a well-established regular, on the Peck Soap Hour. In the next hour the rivalry between Barry and Peck melts in an effort to locate Barbara who is briefly at the mercy of a would-be kidnapper. Jerry and Jimmy arrive shortly before Barry, Margaret, and Peck. All is forgiven, the competitors merge their companies to "wash the neck of the nation" while Barbara, Jerry, and Jimmy dance and sing a slam-bang finish before a large radio audience.

NOTES AND REVIEWS: POOR LITTLE RICH GIRL had been filmed before as a sentimental vehicle for Mary Pickford in 1917. This latter version had not only been updated, it was entirely unrecognizable from its predecessor in that it was specially tailored for the vast audiences of Shirley Temple with plenty of footage devoted to the curly-haired moppet's penchant for song and dance. The result was certainly box office. It was good Temple but a poor vehicle for Faye. It cannot be

With Jack Haley and Shirley Temple.

*With Jack Haley
singing "When I'm With You."*

denied that on such productions *everything* was slanted toward "that Temple child," and while pure and wholesome in appearance and the darling of everyone from Key West to Puget Sound, Shirley was more than a little difficult to work with. Her films commanded big budgets, the finest supporting casts the studio could assemble, and shooting schedules that were a marvel of speed and efficiency. It could not be said that Shirley wasn't a trouper, for she learned her lines (and everyone else's), and she was usually able to film a scene in a single take.

Alice did not make an appearance until the film was almost half over, resulting in less footage than any other of her thirty-three films with the possible exception of NOW I'LL TELL. The promise of KING OF BURLESQUE was not met in this film, but it did offer Alice two of her finest songs: "When I'm With You" and "But Definitely," turned out by Gordon and Revel, a team who would happily supply numbers for future Faye films. The Faye voice was becoming a distinctive asset to a picture. Her deep, throated tones, her natural delivery and warm sincerity

were pertinent features no other screen vocalist came close to emulating.

This first of two Temple-picture assignments was also the second of five stories putting Alice prominently before a radio mike. This was also the first of four Faye films to include Tony Martin, a rising young singer who had an unbilled, thirty-second bit singing "When I'm With You."

But if nothing else the critics were kind: "Alice Faye and Jack Haley, as the song and dance partners, stand out from a sound supporting cast," said *Film Weekly*. "Alice Faye demonstrates that she is worthy of more important assignments," quipped *Daily Variety*.

Fortunately POOR LITTLE RICH GIRL proved to be a Faye milestone in that this was the final film in which Alice's eyebrows were plucked and thinly penciled in. On the way out as well was the platinum blonde hair with its busy marcelled artificiality. The new, more natural, and far lovelier Alice Faye that audiences adored was to rise immediately, and it was a welcome change for everyone.

With Jack Haley and Shirley Temple from the "Military Man" finale production number.

With Jack Haley.

With Jack Haley.

STAR LIGHT, STAR BRIGHT

1936·1939

With the release of SING, BABY, SING the new Alice Faye emerged as if from a restricting cocoon. In this period of three and a half years she worked in no less than thirteen top-budgeted films. It was her most productive period of film making and critical acclaim, and it established her position as a star of the first rank in the Hollywood constellation.

By 1938 IN OLD CHICAGO and ALEXANDER'S RAGTIME BAND had become two of the most important productions of the decade. It was a period of stardom with the best talents in the industry which made her name a valuable commodity to exhibitors everywhere. It was also a period of growing confidence in her own abilities which in turn was reflected in her screen work. The characters she enacted on the screen had become three-dimensional, possessing depth of feeling as well as a fluid self assurance. This was especially noticeable in the above mentioned pictures and to a lesser degree in HOLLYWOOD CAVALCADE, her first Technicolor success. The latter proved that she didn't always have to sing to succeed. But it was the singing roles which endeared her to a growing populace, and the acclaim, such as she had never dreamed possible a few short years before, was now hers to savor and enjoy.

Scripts were now tailored for her, and musical sequences were spotted throughout the proceedings whereby her emotional vocalizing enhanced her own standing—making her more than just another singer. She had developed an intimate vocal quality; she seemingly sang to the individual not to the assembled throng.

Her film titles were a fascinating potpourri on a broad spectrum. One might say: ON THE AVENUE she was destined to WAKE UP AND LIVE, but even if YOU'RE A SWEETHEART, YOU CAN'T HAVE EVERYTHING. She might STOWAWAY as a SALLY or ROSE, only to find that a BARRICADE was really a TAIL SPIN.

As the decade of the 1930's drew to a close, Alice had become a star as bright as any in the heavens. The soft, natural hair falling about her shoulders, the misty eyes big and expressive, and the warmth of that incredible voice had become trademarks no audience could resist.

Sing, Baby, Sing

A 20th Century-Fox Picture 1936
Darryl F. Zanuck In Charge of Production

CAST:

Joan Warren .... ALICE FAYE
Bruce Farraday .... ADOLPHE MENJOU
Nicky .... Gregory Ratoff
Al Craven .... Ted Healy
Fitz .... Patsy Kelly
Ted Blake .... Michael Whalen
Ritz Brothers .... Themselves
Robert Wilson .... Montagu Love
Telephone Operator .... Dixie Dunbar
Mac .... Douglas Fowley
Brewster .... Paul Stanton
Tony Renaldo .... Tony Martin
with:
Virginia Field, Paul McVey, Carol Tevis, Cully Richards, and Lynn Bari.

CREDITS:

Director .... Sidney Lanfield
Associate Producer .... B. G. DeSylva
Screenplay .... Milton Sperling, Jack Yellen
Harry Tugend
Original story .... Milton Sperling
Jack Yellen
Photography .... Peverell Marley, A.S.C.
Art direction .... Mark-Lee Kirk.
Set direction .... Thomas Little
Assistant director .... Fred Fox
Film editor .... Barbara McLean
Costumes .... Royer
Sound .... Arthur Von Kirbach
Roger Heman
Musical director .... Louis Silvers.

Released August 21, 1936. Running time 90 minutes.

SONGS: "Love Will Tell" and "Sing Baby Sing" by Jack Yellen and Lew Pollack; "You Turned the Tables on Me" by Sidney Mitchell and Louis Alter; "When Did You Leave Heaven?" by Walter Bullock and Richard Whiting.

SYNOPSIS: When her singing engagement at Club 41 is cancelled, Joan Warren appeals to her agent Nicky for help. Society girls with blue-blood pedigrees are all the rage for nightclub jobs, and Nicky suggests that Joan's real place is on the radio. Though he succeeds in getting her an audition, Brewster, the station manager, refuses to hire her when he learns she is not one of "the Warrens of Virginia" as Nicky claimed. Later that evening Nicky, his secretary Fitz, and the latter's brother, Al, befriend a very intoxicated Bruce Farraday, and they are present for Joan's final performance at

With chorus—the "Sing, Baby, Sing" number.

the club. Before he passes out and is rushed to the hospital, Bruce, a Hollywood screen idol, fancies that the singing Joan is his Juliet and he Romeo. Ted Blake, hoping to pick up a juicy news item regarding Farraday, hurries to the hospital where Nicky and Al are promising to produce Juliet. Farraday refuses to cooperate until he has had a drink so Al hits upon bay rum as a substitute which Nicky christens "South American Brandy." Bruce loves it, hiding the stuff in a hot water bottle. When Joan and Fitz arrive at the hospital, Bruce is wild with joy, and Ted gets a story and pictures for the evening edition. Using Bruce's name for bait Nicky succeeds in getting a radio offer from Brewster if Farraday will appear with Joan, but before the program can be staged Bruce's cousin, Robert, arrives to take the erratic movie star in tow and get him away from Joan, whom he dubs a gold digger. Bruce and Robert board a train for Hollywood while Ted gets Joan to take up pursuit in a plane. Overtaking Bruce in Kansas City it is decided to hold the proposed broadcast there with local talent and Joan and Bruce as the stars. Everyone succeeds in lining up an act, but Robert returns to see that Bruce does not appear. Ted finally rescues Bruce from Robert's clutches, races with him to the broadcasting studio, and the show, a resounding hit, wins Joan the coveted radio contract.

NOTES AND REVIEWS: Following the credits for SING, BABY, SING this notice, usually relegated to insignificant type at the bottom of the screen, blazed forth in huge letters: "The events and characters depicted in this photoplay are entirely fictional and any similarity with actual persons either living or dead is not intentional but purely coincidental." It was no coincidence that the lead characters in the film were patterned loosely or otherwise on the headline romance of actor John Barrymore and Elaine Barrie, but the result was indeed a happy coincidence for Alice Faye. It was her strongest script to date, giving her a real chance to carry a picture on her own. Critics agreed as is seen in the praise of *Film Weekly* which stated: "Alice Faye, looking much more charming than she has ever done before, carries the burden of the musical numbers, and sings them with a persuasive lilt that is impossible to resist!"

With Michael Whalen.

Alice sang the title song, gave an impressive rendition of "You Turned the Tables on Me" and had one of her loveliest screen numbers of all time in "Love Will Tell." The latter was ruined with interrupting chatter, thereby passing almost unnoticed. The story called for her to discover a young singer working for the city lighting division to whom she gives a chance on the Kansas City broadcast, and Tony Martin's well-mounted number, "When Did You Leave Heaven?" garnered an Academy Award nomination for best song of 1936.

Adolphe Menjou as Bruce was a stroke of brilliant casting. "Be prepared for a new and riotous Adolphe Menjou," said *Photoplay*. "Listen to Alice Faye sing as she never sang before." Though they worked extremely well together and Menjou had one of the best comic roles of his career in SING, BABY, SING, the two never worked together again.

An interesting sidelight was the signing by 20th Century-Fox of Tyrone Power to a studio contract. Alice, sure that Power was box office, volunteered to appear in his screen test and it was she who urged the studio to cast him as Ted Blake. The studio at first agreed and stills for the film exist which bear the name "Tyrone Power, Jr." But at the last moment it was decided that a name was needed and Whalen was rushed into the part after production had been in progress for some time. Alice subsequently starred with Power in three top-budgeted films that most critics agree were among her finest.

Though Alice acted extremely well, sang beautifully, and appeared more natural in her softened hair styles and makeup, the gowns by Royer were atrocious, appearing to be nothing more than pick-me-ups from a bargain basement.

With Patsy Kelly and Michael Whalen.

With Gregory Ratoff, Ted Healy and Patsy Kelly.

With Adolphe Menjou.

With Michael Whalen.

71

Stowaway

A 20th Century-Fox Picture 1936
Darryl F. Zanuck In Charge of Production

CAST:

Ching-Ching	SHIRLEY TEMPLE
Tommy Randall	ROBERT YOUNG
Susan Parker	ALICE FAYE
The Colonel	Eugene Pallette
Mrs. Hope	Helen Westley
Atkins	Arthur Treacher
Judge Booth	J. Edward Bromberg
Kay Swift	Astrid Allwyn
Richard Hope	Allan Lane
Captain	Robert Greig
Chang	Willie Fung
Sun Lo	Philip Ahn

with:
Jayne Regan, Julius Tannen, Paul McVey, Helen Jerome Eddy, William Stack and Honorable Wu.

CREDITS:

Director	William A. Seiter
Producer	B. G. DeSylva
Associate Producers	Earl Carroll
	Harold Wilson
Screenplay	William Conselman, Arthur Sheekman
	Nat Perrin
Story	Samuel G. Engel
Photography	Arthur Miller, A.S.C.
Art decoration	William Darling
Set decorations	Thomas Little
Assistant director	Earl Haley
Film Editor	Lloyd Nosler
Costumes	Royer
Sound	Eugene Grossman
	Roger Heman
Musical director	Louis Silvers

Released December 25, 1936. Running time 87 minutes.

SONGS: "Good Night, My Love," "You Gotta S-m-i-l-e to be H-a-Double-p-y," "One Never Knows, Does One?" by Mack Gordon and Harry Revel, "That's What I Want for Christmas" by Irving Caesar and Gerald Marks.

SYNOPSIS: As blood-thirsty bandits move toward the village of Sanchow in the interior of China, loyal Sun Lo places Ching-Ching, the ward of missionaries, in the custody of Chang and starts her on her way to safety in Shanghai. Once there Chang steals the child's money, and she is left to wander about the bustling city with her dog until she happens upon Tommy Randall, a wealthy playboy on an extended cruise. Seeking refuge from a rain storm Barbara (Ching) hops into the rumble seat of Tommy's roadster and falls asleep. Later, when the car is hoisted aboard ship, the child becomes an inadvertent stowaway. Hours later, with the ship at sea, Barbara starts for the upper decks, makes a noise, and starts a ship-wide search. The frightened child takes refuge in the cabin of Mrs. Hope and Susan Parker, a young woman soon to wed Mrs. Hope's son Richard. Susan befriends Barbara, promises the captain she will be responsible for the child, and thus meets Tommy to whom she is immediately attracted. Susan and Tommy take Barbara ashore at the next port of call where the child enters a Chinese version of a Major Bowes amateur contest. Meddlesome Mrs. Hope, worried by the attention Tommy is paying Susan, wires her son to join them as quickly as possible. Richard comes aboard at the next port, but Susan now finds it hard to take him seriously, knowing she'll always be dominated by Richard's mother. To save Barbara from an orphanage, Susan impulsively marries Tommy, agreeing later to a divorce in which custody of Barbara will fall to Tommy. But in Reno, Judge Booth coaches Barbara for the witness stand, the divorce is called off, and the happy couple spend a joyous Christmas with their daughter in their new home.

With Helen Westley and Shirley Temple.

With Robert Young.

With Shirley Temple and Robert Young.

NOTES AND REVIEWS: STOWAWAY placed Alice in China for the first time in her career. She was, unfortunately, destined for a Chinese setting again. It was her final film with Temple, and if not an entirely happy one, it was her most physically glamorous role to date. It marked her only screen appearance with Robert Young, on loan from Metro Goldwyn Mayer. Her Royer gowns were, for a change, femininely alluring and tastefully simple, while her hair was now a natural blonde allowed to fall naturally about her shoulders in becoming waves. It would not be drastically altered for the next nine years. Undeniably the thoughtful direction of William A. Seiter helped expand her acting range considerably. In short it was truly a new Alice Faye who stepped before the cameras of Arthur Miller. She possessed a quiet dignity and grace — the image was established and would remain with her to the end of her film career.

STOWAWAY was rushed into release so that the film's ending would have a timeliness for the holiday season. Critics agreed that the tacked-on Reno ending was merely an excuse for Shirley's

"That's What I Want for Christmas" number. It played only a few major key cities before the end of 1936, going into general release after the start of 1937.

Alice was given two major songs to sing, placed in a more natural setting to deliver them; they came across with a calm assurance of an artist who seemed to sense that she had found her film footing once and for all. Gone were the cutesie frills of the title song from SING, BABY, SING and the frantic movement never in keeping with the Faye personality. She sang "Goodnight My Love," to Robert Young on a moonlit deck of a ship as they danced romantically. It became one of her biggest selling discs on the Brunswick label. "One Never Knows Does One?" she sang standing alone in the doorway of her stateroom with the moonlight on the China sea behind her; never had a song for her been more perfectly showcased.

"The romantic leads are Robert Young and Alice Faye," said *Variety*." Both very good on performance, particularly Young, and with Miss Faye keeping abreast through her singing."

With Shirley Temple, Robert Young and Allan Lane.

With Shirley Temple, Julius Tannen, Paul McVey and Helen Westley.

With Robert Young.

On the Avenue

A 20th Century-Fox Picture 1937
Darryl F. Zanuck In Charge of Production

CAST:

Gary Blake . . . . DICK POWELL
Mimi Carraway . . . . MADELEINE CARROLL
Mona Merrick . . . . Alice Faye
Ritz Brothers . . . . Themselves
Commodore Carraway . . . . George Barbier
Frederick Sims . . . . Alan Mowbray
Aunt Fritz . . . . Cora Witherspoon
Jake Dibble . . . . Walter Catlett
Eddie Eads . . . . Douglas Fowley
Herman . . . . Stepin Fetchit
Miss Katz . . . . Joan Davis
Herr Hanfstangel . . . . Sig Rumann
Joe Papaloupas . . . . Billy Gilbert
with:
Paul Gerrits, Douglas Wood, Paul Irving, Ricardo Mandia, John Sheehan, E. E. Clive, Harry Stubbs, Edward Cooper, Frank Darien and Lynn Bari

CREDITS:

Director . . . . Roy Del Ruth
Producer . . . . Darryl F. Zanuck
Associate producer . . . . Gene Markey
Screenplay . . . . Gene Markey
                                       William Conselman
Dances staged by . . . . Seymour Felix
Photography . . . . Lucien Andriot, A.S.C.
Art direction . . . . William Darling
   Associate . . . . Mark-Lee Kirk
Set decoration . . . . Thomas Little
Assistant director . . . . William J. Scully
Film editor . . . . Allen McNeil
Costumes . . . . Gwen Wakeling
Sound . . . . Joseph Aiken
                                        Roger Heman
Musical direction . . . . Arthur Lange

Released February 12, 1937. Running time 90 minutes.

SONGS: "He Ain't Got Rhythm," "Slumming on Park Avenue," "The Girl on the Police Gazette," "I've Got My Love to Keep Me Warm," "This Year's Kisses," and "You're Laughing at Me." Music and lyrics by Irving Berlin.

SYNOPSIS: Gary Blake's new show, "On the Avenue" starring Mona Merrick and the Ritz Brothers contains a blunt satire on "The Richest Girl in the World." In the audience Mimi Carraway instantly recognizes herself and is hopping mad. Backstage she is unable to get Gary to drop the skit which she feels makes her

With Dick Powell.

family look foolish. Gary is fascinated by the beautiful Mimi, makes a date with her, and they fall in love. Gary promises Mimi he will "take the sting out of that skit."

Mona, who regards Gary as hers, decides to take matters into her own hands. Making sure that Mimi, her father, Frederick Sims, and Aunt Fritz are in the audience, she changes the material making it worse than before. The result is a disaster, and the Carraways bring suit against Gary. Mimi refuses to speak to Gary, buys the show from producer Jake Dibble, and proceeds to alter the show to make Gary appear foolish, even employing a paid audience to walk out. New York papers are a-buzz with the feud, but Gary is disgusted and tears up his contract, refusing to work for Mimi.

At Mimi's wedding to Arctic explorer Sims, Aunt Fritz steps in and whisks Mimi and Gary away to city hall to be married, and Mona at the finale is making plans to see more of Commodore Carraway.

NOTES AND REVIEWS: Whether due to a strong cast, the Irving Berlin score, or the top-flight production it was, ON THE AVENUE was chosen as the February 1937 attraction for the nation's leading picture house, The Radio City Music Hall. It was Alice's second film to be so honored but one in which she sank to third billing for the second film in a row. Still, it gave her three

With Dick Powell—"I've Got My Love to Keep Me Warm" number.

Irving Berlin songs: "He Ain't Got Rhythm," "Slumming on Park Avenue," and "This Year's Kisses," with which she succeeded in more than holding her own. Musically it was Faye's film all the way, for she appeared in the closing moments of "I've Got My Love to Keep Me Warm" with Powell, and in the "Police Gazette" number she appeared as a brunette for the first of two such screen glimpses (the other was in 1939's HOLLYWOOD CAVALCADE).

"Alice Faye gives another of her thoroughly efficient performances as his (Powell's) jealous stage partner," said *Film Weekly*.

One cannot help but wonder what ON THE AVENUE would have been like had three of Berlin's numbers not been dropped from the release prints. They were: "On the Avenue," "On the Steps of Grant's Tomb," and "Swing Sister," at least two of which featured Faye.

To Lucien Andriot's credit is the superior lighting and photography which made the Faye (and Carroll) closeups moments of lasting beau-

ty. Alice's gowns were skillfully designed, especially the simple black ensemble with the peaked hat.

Oddly enough except for a brief moment in the aforementioned "I've Got My Love to Keep Me Warm" she did not sing with Powell, essentially a Warner Brothers star at this time, and they were never to be teamed again. Diggory Venn's San Francisco review remarked, "Dick Powell is blithe as ever, and goes well with Alice Faye, who given a chance to show off her voice and charm takes it." And Britain's *Picturegoer* wrote, "Alice Faye has a role of a jealous actress which suits her admirably. She brings real character to it, and puts over her song numbers most effectively."

In the opening number, "He Ain't Got Rhythm," playing a chorine is a brief glimpse of Marjorie Weaver, destined to portray Mary in Faye's SALLY, IRENE AND MARY the following year. Lynn Bari had a one-line bit in a nightclub sequence.

78

The "Faye stance"—costume
publicity still
from ON THE AVENUE.

The "Slumming on Park Avenue" number.

With Bess Flowers, Edward Cooper and Madeleine Carroll.

With Stepin Fetchit
and Dick Powell.

Wake Up and Live

A 20th Century-Fox Picture 1937
Darryl F. Zanuck In Charge of Production

With Walter Winchell.

CAST:

Walter Winchell .... HIMSELF
Ben Bernie .... HIMSELF
Alice Huntley .... ALICE FAYE
Patsy Kane .... Patsy Kelly
Steve Cluskey .... Ned Sparks
Eddie Kane .... Jack Haley
Gus Avery .... Walter Catlett
Jean Roberts .... Grace Bradley
Spanish Dancer .... Joan Davis
Cafe Singer .... Leah Ray
James Stratton .... Miles Mander
Herman .... Douglas Fowley
Waldo Peebles .... Etienne Giradot
with:
Barnett Parker, Paul Hurst, Warren Hymer, The Condos Brothers, The Brewster Twins, William Demarest, George Sheehan, George Givot, Ed Gargen, Robert Lowery, Charles Williams, George Chandler, Gary Breckner.

CREDITS:

Director .... Sidney Lanfield
Associate Producer .... Kenneth Macgowan
Screenplay .... Harry Tugend
                                   Jack Yellen
Original story .... Curtis Kenyon
Based upon the book by Dorothea Brande.
Photography .... Edward Cronjager, A.S.C.
Art direction .... Mark-Lee Kirk
Associate .... Haldane Douglas
Set decorations .... Thomas Little
Assistant director .... A. F. Erickson
Film editor .... Robert Simpson
Costumes .... Gwen Wakeling
Sound .... W. D. Flick
                                   Roger Heman
Musical direction .... Louis Silvers.

Released April 23, 1937. Running time 91 minutes.

SONGS: "Wake Up and Live," "Never in a Million Years," "There's A Lull in My Life," "It's Swell of You," "Oh, But I'm Happy," "I Love You Much Too Much, Muchacha," and "I'm Bubbling Over" by Mack Gordon and Harry Revel.

SYNOPSIS: In the midst of a Winchell-Bernie feud which has delighted radio listeners, Eddie Kane and his singing partner, Jean Roberts, arrive in New York eager to crack that elusive nut known as radio broadcasting. Eddie's sister Patsy just happens to be Winchell's Gal Friday, so an audition is arranged for Eddie and Jean. Horrified, Eddie watches as an opera diva passes out cold due to an occupational hazard — mike fright. When it is their turn to audition Eddie freezes up, joining the opera star in the bliss of nirvana. Their radio career over before it has begun, Jean decides to accept a club date while Eddie becomes a tour guide at the broadcasting station and there meets Alice Huntley, the station's "Wake Up and Live" girl whose daily program of inspiration and advice is a popular feature. Alice, feeling sure Eddie can lick his mike fright, starts him singing in front of a dead mike for practice. At one point, due to a mechanical fluke, Eddie's voice goes out over the airwaves accompanied by Bernie's orchestra. The effect is electric. Listeners want the strange singer identified. Bernie christens him "The Phantom Troubador" and on his program tries to pass off another singer for Eddie. Winchell sees through the ruse and exposes the orchestra leader's hoax. The feud is now a nationwide attraction with everyone searching for the Phantom including Patsy's frozen-faced admirer, Steve. Alice, whose own program has been cancelled, promises Stratton that she can deliver the Phantom if the broadcast can be aired from her apartment where Eddie will think he is singing into a dead mike. Gus, alerted by Jean, kidnaps Eddie hoping to sign him as a client. When Eddie's recording is played over the air, Gus

Singing "There's a Lull in My Life."

tears up the contract as worthless. Alice goes on the air to lure Eddie back to her side. Arriving at the club where Bernie is appearing, Eddie, encouraged by Alice, makes the grade. Patsy finally lands the reluctant Steve, Winchell and Bernie shake hands, and Eddie and Alice are destined to be radio's romantic new twosome.

NOTES AND REVIEWS: WAKE UP AND LIVE still remains the best satire on radio ever filmed. The story was another fast, breezy script by Harry Tugend, who would emerge as one of the most frequent scripters of Faye films. It was Faye's third and last picture with Patsy Kelly, and the last time she would ever receive third billing in her career. Joan Davis's Spanish dancer number was a standout comedy gem, Leah Ray was excellent singing "I Love You Much Too Much, Muchacha," and Etienne Giradot in a bit made an audience-participation show memorable as the mistaken Phantom "discovered" by a wildly effeminate Barnet Parker.

Alice, then at the zenith of her recording career (she was one of the only 20th Century-Fox stars to record for a national label — Bruns-

wick), had two fine numbers in the title song and "There's a Lull in My Life," the former a standard always associated with her name. Thomas Little's modernistic sets were the source of much interest, being years ahead of their time and quite similar in mood to another 1937 success, LOST HORIZON.

"Alice Faye gets better and better with each picture," said *Picturegoer.* "She gives a bright performance as the girl who stumbles on the truth." *Film Weekly* noted: "Alice is a sweet heroine and does some charming acting. She plays with charm and her singing is a pure delight." *Film Daily* declared: "Alice Faye, who has never been better photographed, is the love interest opposite Jack."

If script, songs, and photography were in her favor, costumes were not. Gwen Wakeling's mannish suits with their wide lapels were a nightmare of bad taste, by far the poorest worn by Faye in her entire career, making her look mawkish and broader of shoulder than Max Baer. Her hair styles in the closing sequences (20th Century-Fox did not give screen credit for hair styles at that time) were unbecoming in a restricting pompadour roll.

Singing "Wake Up and Live."

With Jack Haley.

With Jack Haley.

With Ben Bernie and Miles Mander.

You Can't Have Everything

A 20th Century-Fox Picture 1937
Darryl F. Zanuck In Charge of Production

CAST:

Judith Poe Wells .... ALICE FAYE
Ritz Brothers .... THEMSELVES
George Macrae .... DON AMECHE
Sam Gordon .... Charles Winninger
Lulu Riley .... Louise Hovick
Rubinoff .... Himself
Bevins .... Arthur Treacher
Bobby Walker .... Tony Martin
Evelyn Moore .... Phyllis Brooks
Jerry .... Wally Vernon
Orchestra Leader .... Louis Prima
with:
Tip, Tap, and Toe (Specialty dancers), George Humbert, Jed Prouty, Dorothy Christy, Clara Blandick.

CREDITS:

Director .... Norman Taurog
Associate Producer .... Laurence Schwab
Screenplay .... Harry Tugend, Jack Yellen,
                                    Karl Tunberg
From an original story by Gregory Ratoff.
Photography .... Lucien Andriot, A.S.C.
Art direction .... Duncan Cramer
Set decorations .... Thomas Little
Assistant director .... Jasper Blystone
Film editor .... Hansen Fritch
Costumes .... Royer
Sound .... Arthur Von Kirbach
                                  Roger Heman
Musical direction .... David Buttolph.

Released August 3, 1937. Running time 100 minutes.

SONGS: "You Can't Have Everything," "Afraid to Dream," "The Loveliness of You," "Please Pardon Us We're in Love," and "Danger — Love at Work" by Mack Gordon and Harry Revel.

SYNOPSIS: Broke and unable to sell her play, NORTH WINDS, Judith orders a double portion of spaghetti knowing she cannot pay for it. After singing to try and pay for her dinner, she is forced to carry a sign advertising the restaurant. Too proud to allow an intoxicated George to pay her check, she unburdens herself to him telling him she sent her play to producer Sam Gordon but has heard nothing. Back at his apartment George is confronted by the furious Lulu whom he stood up earlier that

evening. Next day George and Sam examine Judith's play. It is terrible, but George gets Sam to pay her $250.00 for the rights. In the meantime he sends Lulu off to sunnier climes and convinces his young playwright (who is a granddaughter of Edgar Allen Poe) to take a part in his new musical. When the show opens Lulu returns and informs Judy that George is hers and to lay off or "I'll cut out your heart and stuff it like an olive." Judy, who loves George without reservation, leaves the show and New York behind, returning to her former job — plugging songs in a small-town variety store. Unable to find her, George, who has broken with Lulu, decides to make NORTH WINDS into a musical, sure it will bring Judy back. She discovers the deception when new sheet music comes in proclaiming her literary efforts as a musical. Hurrying to New York where the show is a smash hit on its opening, she and George are reunited.

With Don Ameche.

NOTES AND REVIEWS: In YOU CAN'T HAVE EVERY-
THING Alice's natural charm and warm sincerity were ably molded by director Norman Taurog who was perfectly at home in comedy, musical and dramatic films (IF I HAD A MILLION, BROADWAY MELODY OF 1940, and BOYS' TOWN), Alice here appeared for the first time with Don Ameche, the actor destined to be her perennial costar in no less than six films between 1937 and 1941. Though they were a recognized, popular screen team Ameche lost Alice,

often long before the final reel, in three of their six films. Lacking the virility of a John Payne or a Henry Fonda, Ameche was a serviceable, admittedly well-dressed, suave performer who sang well enough not to eclipse the Faye vocal mellifluence. Alice's vocal prowess was now an admitted asset to any film and one of the main reasons her Fox musicals were such box-office draws. In the *New York Times* on August 2, 1937, Frank S. Nugent conceded that, "Miss Faye continues to be the screen's foremost songplugger. The Gordon and Revel score is facile, probably will be popular and has Miss Faye to put it over."

YOU CAN'T HAVE EVERYTHING also marked the screen debut of Gypsy Rose Lee,

With Paul Hurst.

Singing "Afraid to Dream" with Tony Martin.

billed under her real name, Louise Hovick. The all-powerful code enacted just three years before worried the studio, who feared that the reputation of the world's foremost burlesque queen might upset the delicate balance of good taste in the film capital. It was a ploy which fooled no one. Maury Campbell in his *San Francisco Chronicle* review thought that, "Miss Hovick has what they refer to as a real future in films." Gypsy did have the makings of a caustic, brittle comedy star on the order of Helen Broderick or Eve Arden, but her past overshadowed her work, and the studio never properly handled nor promoted her as an acting talent. Nevertheless, she often got across several cleverly conceived comedy lines seemingly tailored to her own individual style. In a nightclub sequence she happens upon Alice for the first time. Dripping with jewels, swathed in white fox, and with an imperious, disdainful edge to her voice she inquires of Alice, who is dressed in an extremely mannish coat with wide lapels, "Did you get two pair of pants with that suit?"

Upon completion of YOU CAN'T HAVE EVERYTHING Alice Faye and the Ritz Brothers parted company for good. They had had important spots in three Faye films, having been introduced to the screen the year before in Faye's SING, BABY, SING. Also for the third time in a Faye film was rising young singer, Tony Martin, who within the space of a few weeks would make Alice Mrs. Martin. A high point in the picture was their production number duet "Afraid to Dream," a romantic ballad associated with them for a number of years.

But EVERYTHING was everywhere a Faye film. Shortly after the film's start she sang the title song to Rubinoff's violin, did a catchy rendition of "Danger, Love at Work" accompanied by Louis Prima's expressive trumpet, and "Please Pardon Us, We're in Love," one of her finest screen numbers, sung with just the right amount of tenderness at a sheet music counter. *Variety*'s review proclaimed that, "Alice Faye has one of her best parts, and she acts her sentimental scenes with a good deal of sincerity and feeling." *Picturegoer*'s review modestly admitted, "Alice Faye, who, after several years of hard work is gradually climbing to stellar heights, is on top of her form as the playwright."

With Rubinoff singing "You Can't Have Everything."

*With Don Ameche
and Tony Martin.*

You're
A Sweetheart

A Universal Picture 1937
Charles B. Rogers In Charge of Production

CAST:

Betty Bradley	ALICE FAYE
Hal Adams	GEORGE MURPHY
Don King	Ken Murray
'Cherokee' Charlie	Charles Winninger
'Daisy' Day	Andy Devine
Fred Edwards	William Gargan
Harry Howe	Frank Jenks
'Penny' Norris	Frances Hunt
Cousin Casper	Casper Reardon
Oswald	Oswald
Conway Jeeters	Donald Meek

with:
David Oliver, Andrew H. Trimble, Edna Sedgwick, Bob Murphy, Renie Riano, Bobby Watson, and Specialties by: 4 Playboys, Malda and Ray, and Novelle Bros.

CREDITS:

Director	David Butler
Screenplay	Monte Brice
	Charles Grayson
Original story	Warren Wilson, Maxwell Shane,
	William Thomas
Director of photography	George H. Robinson, A.S.C.
Art director	Jack Otterson
Associate	Richard H. Riedel
Film editor	Bernard W. Burton
Musical director	Charles Previn
Dances staged	Carl Randall
Vocal supervision	Charles E. Henderson
Orchestrations	Frank Skinner
Sound	Joseph Lapis
	Bernard B. Brown.

Released December 26, 1937. Running time 96 minutes.

SONGS: "You're A Sweetheart," "Broadway Jamboree," "My Fine Feathered Friend," "Who Killed Maggie?" and "Oh, Oh Oklahoma" by Harold Adamson and Jimmy McHugh. "Scraping the Toast" by Murray Mencher and Charles Tobias. "So It's Love" by Mickey Bloom, Arthur Quenzer and Lou Bring

SYNOPSIS: Following an explosion he labels temperament, Don promises his new musical star, Betty Bradley, that there will be no more corn-ball publicity stunts involving her in promoting his new show. With the show a hit out of town, Don is dismayed to learn that

With Ken Murray.

the Broadway opening conflicts with the big charity benefit for the Milk Fund. But waiter Hal Adams, learning of the problem, suggests Don create interest in the show by making it unavailable to the public for an entire week. Hal thus becomes a 'Texas Oil Baby' who, enamored of Betty, buys up the house for himself. Papers flash the news, and the show seems a hit before it is officially opened. Complications arise when Jeeters suggests Betty get the oilman's name on an advertising contract. At the same time Don is unable to open the show due to outstanding unpaid bills on the costumes and sets. Betty in desperation forges Hal's name to the contract, collects from Jeeters, and gets Don to sign over a half interest in the show to Hal. Jeeters, learning he's been sold a fake signature, threatens to close the show and jail Don and Hal both, but he agrees to wait and see if critic Kenyon Dale likes the show. Daisy and Oswald force the critic to applaud the final curtain, the show clicks, Jeeters is sure to get his money back, and Betty and Hal thus are altar-bound.

The old Faye pose—even in a tree ("My Fine Feathered Friend" number).

Dancing to the title song with George Murphy.

NOTES AND REVIEWS: YOU'RE A SWEET-HEART marked the only film Alice Faye made for Universal, the second and final loan-out from her home studio. The result was a fortunate blend of comedy, excellent songs (who can forget Faye leaning against a pillar and in her throaty manner declare "So It's Love?"), a fast-paced script, and simple yet elegantly styled gowns of basic black or silver. In addition, Alice worked well with Murphy as evidenced by the clever dance number to the title song in which they proceeded from the stage, up the side of the auditorium, across the balcony, and a flashy return to the stage. *Variety* declared, "Miss Faye has added fancy ballroom dancing to her versatile equipment, and Murphy has acquired a rather pleasing singing voice on top of his dancing skill. That gives the two a chance for superlative teamwork in every department."

Beautifully coiffured (again no screen credit was given) Alice photographed superbly from a variety of angles giving her face a becoming three-dimensional depth not always achieved previously.

The finale number, "Who Killed Maggie?" was a swing version of the vintage tune, "When You and I Were Young, Maggie," here given a courtroom setting and some snappy talked-sung lyrics perfectly in keeping with the times. Faye's opening number in the film, "My Fine Feathered Friend," is best forgotten. Perched in a stage tree only slightly smaller than a giant redwood, she was dressed in a feathered costume and forced to chirp in bird language.

Universal, realizing the drawing power of their star, rushed SWEETHEART into Christmas release, thus getting the jump on 20th Century-Fox who had completed their epic, IN OLD CHICAGO, but were still editing to a reasonable running time. As Diggory Venn, writing in the Christmas issue of his San Francisco column declared without reservations, "New Universal's Christmas present to the world is Alice Faye. The glamorous screen and radio star displays her charms in 'You're a Sweetheart,' which opened yesterday at the Orpheum Theatre. The point being that Miss Faye is very attractive. Her singing is merely adequate on the ether waves, but the magicians have got to work on the sound tracks and on the screen her voice is grand. The picture is invested with some catchy tunes such as 'You're a Sweetheart' and 'So It's Love' and when the aforesaid Alice puts them over with her dreamy eyes, that's enough."

With Ken Murray,
George Murphy
(Alice in costume for the
"Who Killed Maggie?"
number)
and Frank Jenks.

With Donald Meek.

With Ken Murray, George Murphy,
Frances Hunt and Andy Devine.

Sally, Irene, and Mary

A 20th Century-Fox Picture 1938
Darryl F. Zanuck In Charge of Production

With Fred Allen.

CAST:

Sally Day	ALICE FAYE
Tommy Randall	TONY MARTIN
Gabriel (Gabby) Green	FRED ALLEN
Jefferson Twitchell	JIMMY DURANTE
Irene Keene	JOAN DAVIS
Baron Zorka	Gregory Ratoff
Mary Stevens	Marjorie Weaver
Joyce Taylor	Louise Hovick
Oscar	Barnett Parker
Miss Barkow	Mary Treen

with:
J. Edward Bromberg, Eddie Collins, Andrew Tombes, Charles Wilson, The Brian Sisters and the Raymond Scott Quintet.

CREDITS:

Director	William A. Seiter
Associate Producer	Gene Markey
Screen play	Harry Tugend
	Jack Yellen
Original story	Karl Tunberg
	Don Ettinger
Suggested by the stage play by	Edward Dowling
	Cyrus Wood
Dances staged	Nick Castle
	Geneva Sawyer
Photography	Peverell Marley, A.S.C.
Art direction	Bernard Herzbrun
	Rudolph Sternad
Set decoration	Thomas Little
Film editor	Walter Thompson
Costumes	Gwen Wakeling
Sound	Arthur Von Kirbach
	Roger Heman
Musical director	Arthur Lange

Released March 4, 1938. Running time 86 minutes.

SONGS: "Got My Mind on Music," and "Sweet as a Song" by Mack Gordon and Harry Revel. "Minuet in Jazz" by Raymond Scott. "Half Moon on the Hudson," "I Could Use a Dream," "This Is Where I Came In," "Who Stole the Jam?" and "Help Wanted: Male" by Walter Bullock and Harold Spina. "Hot Potata" by Jimmy Durante

SYNOPSIS: Sally, Irene, and Mary are manicurists par excellence in the tonsorial parlor of Oscar, but their minds are on Broadway careers. The girls get a chance to sing for Baron Zorka, but following an argument with Gabby, their agent, the Baron demolishes the establishment. Gabby quickly gets them non-singing jobs at the Covered Wagon in the Village where the girls meet Tommy, the club's singer. Gabby induces the wealthy widow, Joyce, to invest in a show to star Tommy and the girls. But the green-eyed monster of jealousy bites Joyce who fears that the relationship of Tommy and Sally is just too cozy. She demands Sally be fired, so Tommy quits too. Down to their last can of beans Mary suddenly is informed that a wealthy uncle has died leaving her a steamship line. The "line" proves to be a rotting hulk of a ferry known as the *General Fremont*. Gabby declares that with $25,000 they can turn the vessel into a showboat-restaurant. Sally agrees to marry the Baron, and Tommy accepts Joyce's offer of marriage each for a fee of $25,000. Gabby and his partner Twitchell, a former sanitation "engineer," turn the *Fremont* into a classy supper club with Sally and Tommy slated for the opening show. During the show on opening night Twitchell, who is sent below to stoke the furnace, sets the ship's gears in motion so that the old tub breaks her moorings and heads into the shipping lanes. Order is finally restored, the guests are again seated at their tables, and the show proceeds as the ship is towed back to her berth. In the show's final moments the captain marries Sally and Tommy. The show is a hit, Joyce and the Baron will realize a tidy profit on their investment and a happy Baron Zorka informs the bejeweled Joyce he, "Will send for your trunks in the morning."

With Joan Davis.

With Marjorie Weaver and Joan Davis singing "Got My Mind on Music".

NOTES AND REVIEWS: Filmed as a silent in 1 9 2 5 SALLY, IRENE, AND MARY was long on drama with the title roles filled by Constance Bennett, Joan Crawford and Sally O'Neil. The Faye-Davis-Weaver version bore little resemblance to the first film nor the play that preceded it. This latter version was another in the snappy, fast-paced musicals typical of the times which rang a happy tune at the box-office if not always an enthusiastic response from the critics. "Played more 'straight' and shorn of some of its more extravagant moments, it would have been a first-rate musical comedy-romance," thought *Film Weekly.*

The studio capitalized on the fact that the film's stars, Faye and Martin, were Mr. and Mrs. off screen. "Positively the Top Hit Ever Given You by 'Hit Maker' Darryl F. Zanuck!!!" read the ads. Frank Nugent, writing in the *New York Times,* didn't agree. "It is a forthright exploitation of the voice, full lips and other things of Alice Faye and her tenor-husband, Tony Martin, and it goes about this simple little chore with commendable directness. Speaking personally, we've had enough close-ups of the luscious Miss Faye, whose inability to speak or sing without throwing her mouth into trembles has begun to wear us down."

Following the release of this picture Faye and Martin never again appeared in a film together. The high hopes of Marjorie Weaver for stardom did, however, not materialize though she made almost twenty more films for Fox, mostly second leads and roles in a string of undistinguished B's.

SALLY, IRENE AND MARY had the distinction of being the first feature film to include a Big Apple sequence. "Who Stole the Jam?" is thus historic but not necessarily memorable. Another number, "Think Twice," was cut before release and is now regarded as a "lost Faye number" existing today only in a few tape collections. Also Alice's dance sequences in the "Minuet in Jazz" number and the entire number "Half Moon on the Hudson" which she did with Martin on a balcony of their rooming house were cut from subsequent television prints. The latter number exists today only as a brief finale number at the close of the film.

Faye's best musical number was the plaintive "This Is Where I Came In" delivered almost entirely in closeup on the deck of the *Fremont.* It set a pattern in that most of Alice's better numbers in future films were done almost entirely in closeup.

With Gregory Ratoff.

With Tony Martin.

With Marjorie Weaver and Joan Davis.

In Old Chicago

A 20th Century-Fox Picture 1938
A Darryl F. Zanuck Production

CAST:

Dion O'Leary	TYRONE POWER
Belle Fawcett	ALICE FAYE
Jack O'Leary	DON AMECHE
Molly O'Leary	Alice Brady
Pickle Bixby	Andy Devine
Gil Warren	Brian Donlevy
Ann Colby	Phyllis Brooks
Bob O'Leary	Tom Brown
Hattie	Madame Sultewan
Senator Colby	Berton Churchill
General Sheridan	Sidney Blackmer
Gretchen	June Storey

with:

Paul Hurst, J. Anthony Hughes, Gene Reynolds, Bobs Watson, Billy Watson, Spencer Charters, Russell Hicks, Rondo Hatton, Thelma Manning, Eddie Collins, Joe Twerp, Clarence Hummel Wilson, Gustav von Seyffertitz.

CREDITS:

Director	Henry King
Screenplay	Lamar Trotti
	Sonya Levien
Original story	Niven Busch
Special effects director	H. Bruce Humberstone
Special effects scenes	Fred Sersen, Ralph Hammeras,
	Louis J. Witte
Special effects photographer	
	Daniel B. Clarke, A.S.C.
Photographer	Peverell Marley, A.S.C.
Art direction	William Darling
	Rudolph Sternad
Set decoration	Thomas Little
Unit manager	Booth McCracken
Assistant director	Robert Webb
Editor	Barbara McLean
Costumes	Royer
Sound	Eugene Grossman
	Roger Heman
Musical director	Louis Silvers
Associate producer	Kenneth MacGowan

Released April 15, 1938. Running time 115 minutes.

SONGS: "In Old Chicago" by Mack Gordon and Harry Revel. "I'll Never Let You Cry," "I've Taken a Fancy to You," and "Take a Dip in the Sea" by Sidney Clare and Lew Pollack. "Carry Me Back to Old Virginny" by James A. Bland.

SYNOPSIS: Molly O'Leary, left a widow with three small sons, takes in washing in Chicago. As the years pass, Jack, the eldest, becomes a budding lawyer; Dion interests himself in gambling and politics, while Bob drives

Receiving direction on the set.

the laundry wagon. In Gil Warren's saloon Dion meets and becomes interested in Belle Fawcett, a singer Warren has imported from New York. He makes an immediate play for Belle, who at first repulses his advances, but she proves no match for his powers of persuasion, especially when Dion wants to build a place to outdo Warren. As Jack begins to win cases and acquire a name for himself as an honest man, Dion and Belle's Senate is opened and proves to be a big success. Warren, instead of trying to compete, announces that he plans to run for mayor and asks for Dion's support, even going so far as presenting Dion with a check for $10,000. Belle reproaches Dion for this latest move, but Dion has other thoughts. He has some of his henchmen approach Jack about running for mayor; the unsuspecting Jack accepts. Warren seems sure to be elected, but Dion frames a plot at a pre-election rally and has his men start a fight with Warren's. Thus all of Warren's vote repeaters land in jail as the honest people of Chicago elect Jack. Later when Jack tries to clean up the Patch using Belle as a witness against Dion's corrupt ways, Dion beguiles Belle into marriage which Jack performs in his office. Now his wife, Belle cannot testify against her husband as Dion points out. Jack and Dion fight in the mayor's office as Belle prepares to leave the city. Mrs. O'Leary, hearing of the fight, forgets to put the bar between the cow's legs, and the cow upsets a lantern starting one of history's greatest fires. Jack mobilizes the city's fire fighters and uses the army under General Sheridan to start a firebreak using dynamite to blow up buildings. In a

Singing "Carry Me Back to Old Virginny"
(note distinctive Faye pose.)

clash with Warren's men Jack and Pickle are killed as an exploding building buries them. Warren is killed in a stampede of cattle from the stock yards. Dion and Tom search the lake front for Mrs. O'Leary and Tom's wife Gretchen. Belle, who helped rescue Mrs. O'Leary, is reunited with Dion as Chicago burns dramatically in the background.

NOTES AND REVIEWS: IN OLD CHICAGO, a pet project of producer Darryl F. Zanuck, was the third in a series of four great disaster films to reach the screen in the late thirties (SAN FRANCISCO, M-G-M 1936; THE HURRICANE, Samuel Goldwyn 1937; IN OLD CHICAGO, 20th Century-Fox 1938; and THE RAINS CAME, 20th Century-Fox 1939). With a production budget of $1,800,000 it was one of the decade's biggest productions; its twenty-minute climactic fire sequence has never been equalled. So great was the danger considered to be that during the actual shooting of the fire on the back lot, no women were allowed on the set. Men dressed in long skirts and bonnets doubled for the women called for in the script. Actually filmed in 1937 prior to Alice's loan-out to Universal for YOU'RE A SWEETHEART, it was held up for release while every attention was paid to painstaking editing and sound recording for the fire sequences. The film garnered six Academy Award nominations (released in 1938 it strangely competed in the 1937 balloting) including best picture and won two: Alice Brady as Best Supporting Actress and Robert Webb as Assistant Director (the latter award was not given after 1937).

The role of Belle was originally intended for Jean Harlow, whom Fox hoped to obtain from M-G-M by a loan-out agreement. Following her untimely death in mid-1937 director Henry King personally asked for Alice. They worked well together, and Faye credits King with giving her career the acceleration that resulted in her becoming a top screen star and big-name, box-office draw.

Alice starred opposite Tyrone Power for the first time, even taking second billing to him, an honor bestowed upon no other star in her subsequent films. Her numbers were well mounted and expertly tailored to her vocal styling, especially the title number. It was her first time in period costumes, and Royer's gowns were expertly designed to compliment her figure. For her number "Carry Me Back to Old Virginny" Alice wore the famous $1,500 pair of jeweled stockings she had worn for a short sequence in ON THE AVENUE. This time the press made much of them, and the Faye legs became famous.

W. H. Mooring, writing in *Film Weekly*, said: "For his experiment with a more dramatic Alice Faye, Zanuck combined wisdom and daring. He knew Alice Faye could be induced to act, but he expected her public would still wish her to sing ... so sing she does, in Tyrone Power's old-time Chicago gin parlour."

Film Daily stated: "Alice Faye is decorative and capable as the chief entertainer in Power's saloon, who has torrid and tempestuous love scenes with Power, her sweetheart."

With Tyrone Power.

Giving Mrs. O'Leary (Alice Brady) the will to go on.

With Tyrone Power
and Alice Brady.

With Don Ameche, Tyrone Power, Harry Hayden,
Nora Cecil and Charles Williams.

Alexander's Ragtime Band

A 20th Century-Fox Picture 1938
Darryl F. Zanuck in charge of production

With Ethel Merman.

CAST:

Roger Grant (Alexander)	TYRONE POWER
Stella Kirby	ALICE FAYE
Charlie Dwyer	DON AMECHE
Jerry Allen	Ethel Merman
Davey Lane	Jack Haley
Professor Heinrich	Jean Hersholt
Aunt Sophie	Helen Westley
Taxi Driver	John Carradine
Bill	Paul Hurst
Wally Vernon	Himself
Ruby	Ruth Terry
Snapper	Douglas Fowley
Louie	Chick Chandler
Corporal Collins	Eddie Collins
Charles Dillingham	Joe King

with:
Joseph Crehan, Robert Gleckler, Dixie Dunbar, Charles Coleman, Stanley Andrews, Charles Williams, Selmar Jackson, Tyler Brooke, Donald Douglas, Jane Jones, Otto Fries and Mel Kalish.

CREDITS:

Director	Henry King
Associate Producer	Harry Joe Brown
Screen Play	Kathryn Scola
	Lamar Trotti
Adaptation	Richard Sherman
Musical director	Alfred Newman
Dances staged	Seymour Felix
Photography	Peverell Marley, A.S.C.
Art direction	Bernard Herzbrun
	Boris Leven
Set decorations	Thomas Little
Film editor	Barbara McLean
Costumes	Gwen Wakeling
Sound	Arthur von Kirbach
	Roger Heman

Released August 19, 1938. Running time 105 minutes.

SONGS: Old songs actually sung in the film: "Alexander's Ragtime Band," "Ragtime Violin," "That International Rag," "Everybody's Doing It Now," "This Is the Life," "When the Midnight Choo-Choo Leaves for Alabam'," "For Your Country and My Country," "I Can Always Find a Little Sunshine at the YMCA," "Oh! How I Hate to Get Up in the Morning," "We're on Our Way to France," "Say It with Music," "A Pretty Girl Is Like a Melody," "Blue Skies," "Pack Up Your Sins and Go to the Devil," "What'll I Do?" "Remember," "Everybody Step," "All Alone," "Gypsy in Me," "Easter Parade," "Heat Wave."

Instrumental or background: "Cheek to Cheek," "Lazy," "Marie," "Some Sunny Day," "The Song Is Ended," "When I Lost You."

New songs written for this film: "Now It Can Be Told," "I'm Marching Along with Time," "My Walking Stick."

Music and lyrics by Irving Berlin.

SYNOPSIS: It is 1915 and young Roger Grant of aristocratic Nob Hill disappoints his Aunt Sophie and Professor Heinrich when he abandons classical music for the popular ragtime played on San Francisco's Barbary Coast. Roger and his band obtain a job on the coast playing "Alexander's Ragtime Band," a new tune Stella Kirby left on the bar. Flamboyant Stella reluctantly joins Roger whom she dubs a stuck-up snob.

In a short time Alexander and his Ragtime Band are the hottest hit in town, but Stella is convinced their success depends on her voice alone. Under the tutelage of Roger, Stella tones down her flashy, floozie-like feathers and beads to become a beautiful, natural blonde who is gradually falling in love with Roger. Now a permanent fixture at the fashionable Cliff House, they get visiting New York producer, Charles Dillingham, to hear their music, sure he will offer them a contract. Dillingham likes what he hears, but he is only interested in Stella. Charlie

With Jack Haley, Don Ameche and Tyrone Power (singing title song.)

Singing "Now It Can Be Told" (Ty Power to the right.)

urges Stella to accept the New York offer, bringing about a quarrel with Roger.

She departs for a successful career in the East. When the U.S. enters World War I, Roger enlists and is placed in charge of an army show which briefly plays Broadway. Stella is in the audience eager to make up with Roger, but the cast departs for France marching out of the theatre and to the waiting transports.

Stella marries Charlie, now a brilliant song writer, and becomes Broadway's most sought-after star. When the war ends and Roger returns she realizes her love for him. She and Charlie agree to an amiable divorce, but Roger is unaware of this.

Roger hires Jerry, a young vocalist with a powerful voice, and their rise is swift. Later in Paris, Roger admits he cannot ever love Jerry. When the band returns in triumph to the States, Stella has dropped from sight. Disillusioned and alone she has been singing one-night stands carrying a torch for Roger until she happens into Bill's speakeasy in New York on the eve of Roger's Carnegie Hall debut.

A kindly cab driver who recognizes Stella takes her to the concert, and she watches from the wings backstage until Roger spots her and pulls her on stage to reprise their most famous number, "Alexander's Ragtime Band." The swing concert convinces even Aunt Sophie and Professor Heinrich that the new music has merit. Stella and Roger are thus happily reunited.

NOTES AND REVIEWS: ALEXANDER'S RAGTIME BAND was a milestone in film production for 1938. It was, all told, in production for two years. The Academy of Motion Picture Arts and Sciences nominated it for a total of six Oscars including Best Picture. (See appendix — Academy Awards.) It had a two-million-dollar budget, was entrusted to Henry King, one of Hollywood's top directors, and had the added distinction of containing nearly 30 songs all by Irving Berlin, America's leading popular music composer. The picture boasted proudly of eighty-five huge sets, one of which had seven 1500-pound chandeliers of cut glass hand made in Czechoslovakia. So important was the film that it is still included on the *International Motion Picture Almanac*'s list of "The Great Hundred," the most widely ac-

With Don Ameche.

cepted list of the finest feature films ever produced. In addition it made virtually every list of the ten best films of 1938.

With the production of ALEXANDER'S RAGTIME BAND, the musical film gained new status; it was lifted from the ranks of trite backstage stories to a respectable place of honor and prestige. It was the coming of age for musical films both in America and abroad. Most importantly it proved that Alice Faye was an actress and not merely a song plugger. "The film is a triumph for Alice Faye," proclaimed *Film Weekly*. Later the same publication corrected itself by saying, "It is the splendid sincerity of Alice Faye which gives the film its sentimental purpose."

It was undeniably sentimental, but it was not old fashioned. It skillfully reflected the twenty-two years (1915-1938) change in popular music from the honky-tonk era through the years of radio broadcasting. Zanuck, however, would not allow his stars to age in the process, so as the *New York Times* pointed out, "Miss Faye and Tyrone Power go through the years without getting a gray hair or a wrinkle." If the Gwen Wakeling costumes of earlier Faye pictures had been undistinguished, those for ALEXANDER'S RAGTIME BAND more than made up for past oversights. The gowns worn by even the res-

taurant and theatre extras were beguilingly feminine and perfectly in keeping with the period.

In addition to his standards and favorites included in the score Berlin wrote "Now It Can Be Told" especially for Alice to introduce, and then went on record as saying "I'd rather have Alice Faye introduce my songs than any other singer I know." "Miss Faye, in coaxing voice, shares the hotter ditties with shouting Ethel Merman, and a new ballad, 'Now It Can Be Told' with Mr. Ameche. Only one era could have produced ALEXANDER'S RAGTIME BAND — and you're part of it," declared a satisfied Philip K. Scheuer in *Picture Play*.

Again Alice took second billing to Tyrone Power, the fastest rising male star in Hollywood. Though Power appeared in more footage than Faye it was to remain one of her personal favorites. "The role itself was unusual," stated Alice in an interview years later. "It really was two roles in one. In the first half of the picture, Stella behaved at times like a little tough and wore rather flashy clothes. In the second half her roughness had been smoothed away and her clothes toned down. At all times she was essentially kind but quick-tempered and outspoken. She must have been quite a person, for I have seen many films since which tried to recapture the spirit and personality of just such a character. So I'm glad that I played Stella Kirby."

Tail Spin

A 20th Century-Fox Picture 1939
Darryl F. Zanuck in Charge of Production

With Joan Davis, Constance Bennett and Charles Farrell.

CAST:

Trixie Lee	ALICE FAYE
Gerry Lester	CONSTANCE BENNETT
Lois Allen	NANCY KELLY
Babe Dugan	Joan Davis
Bud	Charles Farrell
Alabama	Jane Wyman
Dick (TEX) Price	Kane Richmond
Chick	Wally Vernon
Sunny	Joan Valerie
Speed Allen	Edward Norris
Al Moore	J. Anthony Hughes
T. P. Lester	Harry Davenport
Mrs. Lee	Mary Gordon
Cafe Manager	Harry Rosenthal
Storekeeper	Irving Bacon
Announcer	Sam Hayes

CREDITS:

Director	Roy Del Ruth
Associate Producer	Harry Joe Brown
Screen play	Frank Wead
Photography	Karl Freund, A.S.C.
Art direction	Bernard Herzbrun
	Rudolph Sternad
Set decorations	Thomas Little
Film editor	Allen McNeil
Costumes	Gwen Wakeling
Sound	Eugene Grossman
	Roger Heman
Technical directors	Paul Mantz
	Clifford W. Henderson
Musical direction	Louis Silvers

Released February 19, 1939. Running time 84 minutes.

SONG: "Are You in the Mood for Mischief?" by Mack Gordon and Harry Revel.

SYNOPSIS: Flying enthusiasts Trixie and Babe pool their limited cash and enter the Powder Puff Derby, a cross-country race from Los Angeles to Cleveland where they plan to enter the annual air meet. Flying solo and just short of the race's climax, Trixie's ship develops an oil leak and she cracks up.

After her ship is towed to Cleveland, Bud commences work on the plane to ready it for the meet, but time, parts, and labor are not available so Trixie cons the airport storekeeper into letting her have the parts she needs by promising to cut him in on her prize money. She then induces Naval Lieutenant Price to lend her a couple of his men to ready her plane in time for the competition. That night at a party for flyers Trixie has reason to think Tex is romantically interested in her.

All is friendly rivalry between Trixie, Lois, Alabama, and Sunny until the arrival of wealthy Gerry Lester, who comes to the meet with two fast, modern ships. Thinking her a showoff Alabama takes to the air to show the upstart some real flying. Falling into Gerry's slip stream Alabama crashes. Her plane is a total loss and her injuries put her out of the running for the competition. Babe later separates Trixie and Gerry who have descended to a slapping, hair-pulling brawl.

Gerry, realizing she hasn't the experience for speed flying, offers her plane to Lois's husband, Speed. Lois and Speed are delighted at the chance to try for the prize money, but the plane is faulty and Speed crashes and is killed. Lois is heart-broken, and early next morning takes her ship up followed in close pursuit by Trixie who tries to signal the determined girl to land. Lois crashes her ship in a tail spin.

Trixie flies in the parachute jump and Babe wins a top prize for her jump. Then in an endurance run before a record crowd Gerry pulls out of the race leaving Trixie a clear field for the trophy. Gerry's plane, however, develops engine trouble and she is forced to bail out. Her parachute fouls and she is injured. Trixie visits Gerry in the hospital, their differences forgotten in their zest for the flight game they both love. Outside Gerry's room Trixie bids Tex farewell, realizing he really loves Gerry. With her name blazing from the headlines, Trixie and Babe start home when Trixie gets a job offer from a leading oil company and at the last moment takes Bud along as her personal mechanic.

With Kane Richmond singing "Are You in the Mood for Mischief?"

With Jane Wyman and Joan Valerie.

With Joan Valerie, Nancy Kelly, Joan Davis, Jane Wyman and Jonathan Hale.

With Kane Richmond.

TAIL SPIN was an anachronism in Alice's film career and a role seemingly unsuited to the image she had successfully built up as a romantic chanteuse. She was forced to appear extremely masculine in flying suits (though in one sequence she flew her plane in pursuit of suicide-bound Kelly dressed in flaring skirt and heels) and the script allowed her only two chaste kisses and no romance. While seemingly out of place in a plane cockpit, she went through the motions with determined zest aided by clever studio tricks in flying, though none of the principals ever left the ground. The aerial photography of Karl Freund was often original though rear projection was frequently employed and process work was much in evidence.

The screen play was the work of former U.S. Navy commander Frank Wead, noted for his intelligent scripts for "Dirigible," "Hell Divers," "Ceiling Zero," and "Dive Bomber." Footage from the Cleveland Air Meet of 1938 was actually incorporated in the footage utilizing some of the most modern planes of the day.

Alice recorded two songs for TAIL SPIN, but only one, "Are You in the Mood for Mischief?" ended up in the footage. It is a number largely forgotten today, but it ranks as a fine number ideally suited to the familiar throaty delivery she excelled at. It was beautifully staged between plane crashes on the terrace of the club where she sang to Kane Richmond midway through the proceedings. The other number, "Go In and Out the Window" apparently exists today only on an obscure 20th Century-Fox studio recording. It consists of obviously drunken revelry on the part of the vocalists with only a chorus of non-sense lyrics going to Alice. The film undoubtedly benefited by its being dropped.

The role of Gerry Lester had originally been slated for Loretta Young; Connie Bennett enacted the part. Her sophistication and self assurance gave Alice some strong competition. Kelly was allowed to shamelessly overact with a dripping brand of sweetness which must stand as a record of saccharine slush not equalled outside of a poverty row B film. Charles Farrell was entirely wasted in a nothing part of a mechanic who did little more than grip a wrench and frown. Joan Davis's comic possibilities weren't employed to their fullest, but some of her lines fell just short

With Constance Bennett.

of classic. At one point she shows up on the field obviously intoxicated. Asked where she has been she replied, "Out shavin' a lion!" Though his name appeared on all advertising posters and stills, Warren Hymer's role was entirely deleted from the footage.

"Alice Faye has a poor role, but managed to survive," said *Photoplay.* "Joan Davis and Wally Vernon work at starchy comedy."

The *New York Times* reported, "It is constructed on a simple formula: every time the picture is about to crash, Mr. Zanuck crashes a couple of planes instead. And though in retrospect the story seems to be strewn with the wreckage from these artistic emergencies, what possible solution to any dramatic imbroglio could be quicker and cleaner to the participants, more exciting or more spectacular to the onlookers than a good old-fashioned plane crash. Miss Faye is a girl flyer who has to enter transcontinental air derbies to make a living — and with that voice, too."

Rose of Washington Square

A 20th Century-Fox Picture 1939
Darryl F. Zanuck In Charge of Production

With Tyrone Power (in costume for the "My Man" number.)

CAST:

Bart Clinton	TYRONE POWER
Rose Sargent	ALICE FAYE
Ted Cotter	AL JOLSON
Harry Long	William Frawley
Peggy	Joyce Compton
Whitey Boone	Hobart Cavanaugh
Buck Russell	Moroni Olsen
Barouche Driver	E. E. Clive
Band Leader	Louis Prima
Mike Cavanaugh	Charles Wilson
Chumps	Hal K. Dawson
	Paul Burns
Toby	Ben Welden
Irving	Horace MacMahon
District Attorney	Paul Stanton
Dexter	Harry Hayden
Judge	John Hamilton

CREDITS:

Director	Gregory Ratoff
Associate Producer	Nunnally Johnson
Screen Play	Nunnally Johnson
Based on a story by John Larkin and Jerry Horwin.	
Dances	Seymour Felix
Photography	Karl Freund, A.S.C.
Art direction	Richard Day
	Rudolph Sternad
Set decoration	Thomas Little
Film editor	Louis Loeffler
Costumes	Royer
Sound	Eugene Grossman
	Roger Heman
Musical direction	Louis Silvers

Released May 5, 1939. Running time 86 minutes.

SONGS: "I Never Knew Heaven Could Speak" by Mack Gordon and Harry Revel, "Rose of Washington Square" by James F. Hanley and Ballard MacDonald, "I'm Always Chasing Rainbows" by Harry Carroll and Joe McCarthy, "My Man" by Maurice Yvain, A. Willemetz, and Jacques Charles (English lyrics by Channing Pollack), "Toot, Toot, Tootsie (Goodbye)" by Gus Kahn and Ernie Erdman, "The Curse of an Aching Heart" by Al Piantadosi and Henry Fink, "I'm Sorry I Made You Cry" by N. J. Clesi, "The Vamp" by Byron Gay, "California, Here I Come" by B. G. DeSylva, Joseph Meyer, and Al Jolson, "My Mammy" by Joe Young, Sam Lewis, and Walter Donaldson, "Pretty Baby" by Tony Jackson and Egbert Van Alstyne, "Ja-Da" by Bob Carleton, "Rock-a-bye Your Baby with a Dixie Melody" by Jean Schwartz, Sam M. Lewis, and Joe Young, "I'm Just Wild About Harry" by Noble Sissle and Eubie Blake.

SYNOPSIS: As the 1920's roar into high gear, Rose Sargent finds herself reduced to singing at amateur nights for nickels and dimes. Disgusted, she and Peggy register for a holiday in a Long Island resort. Here Rose meets handsome Bart Clinton, irresponsible get-rich-quick artist, who takes her to a party at the home of his former commander, Buck Russell. The evening turns sour for all when Bart's latest scheme backfires. An expensive necklace is delivered to him with a detective in hot pursuit. Without a word to Rose, Bart skips out and disappears.

Meanwhile, in New York, Rose's former partner, Ted Cotter, gets a chance to appear before some important producers. His act, enlivened inadvertently by an intoxicated loud-mouth in a box, is a hit and Ted and the drunk, hastily rechristened Whitey Boone, are signed for a show.

Back in New York, Rose is singing at a basement speakeasy where Bart brings some pals. When the police stage a raid, Bart takes her out as his guest, and their love blooms anew. At a backstage party for Ted, Rose sings a song at-

The Havana honeymoon scene with Tyrone Power.

With male chorus singing the title song.

tracting the attention of agent Harry Long. Bart, always on the ropes financially, sells his non-existent contract as Rose's representative to Harry. Cotter suspects Bart who wiggles out of the situation by selling the expensive furniture in the apartment he occupies while the owner is in Europe. Bart and Rose marry and go to Havana on their honeymoon. Their happiness is complete when a cablegram announces that Rose has been given a spot in the new edition of Ziegfeld's Follies.

In New York Rose is a sensation, but Bart has his back against a beckoning jail cell when he is confronted by an irate Dexter, who demands that Bart hand over the money he got for the furniture. Desperate for the cash, Bart becomes involved in a crime ring, goes out on a big robbery job and is caught. Ted posts bail, but the newspapers make Rose and Bart miserable with their lurid stories. Bart in desperation skips town as Rose becomes a sensation on stage nightly pouring out her heart singing "My Man."

Broke, alone and discouraged, Bart finally hears the song from a seat in the gallery. He gives himself up, pleads guilty, and is sentenced to five years in Sing Sing. At the gates of Grand Central Station Rose bids Bart farewell, tearfully promising to wait for him.

NOTES AND REVIEWS: Once again as they had done with SING, BABY, SING the producers claimed that ROSE OF WASHINGTON SQUARE was "entirely fictional and any similarity with actual persons either living or dead is not intentional but purely coincidental." Fanny Brice thought it something more than coincidental, and the story contained more fact than fiction — striking alarmingly close to home. She sued the studio claiming that it was her life story thus depicted. The studio quietly settled out of court and ROSE was a success.

It was the final teaming of Tyrone Power with Alice Faye, a screen team many were convinced were wed in real life. It was to remain one of the most remembered Faye roles, possessing a meaty story with a different twist and an abundance of memorable music.

With Al Jolson.

The production had a gloss typical of 20th Century-Fox's craftsmanship which ranked with the best Hollywood could offer. Ratoff, never known as a leading director, was capable and even original. But Royer, again in charge of costumes, failed dismally. The 1920's gowns were typically 1939 modern, for Fox somehow seemed incapable of keeping to the period in either this or Alice's next film, HOLLYWOOD CAVALCADE. It wasn't until 1943 with Ginger Rogers' nearly perfect ROXIE HART that the studio managed twenties costumes. It is ironic that ROXIE had been bought for Faye originally. It would have been interesting to see how Alice would have handled the wise-cracking, gum-chewing bird brain.

Again the demands of double-billing necessitated trimming the running time and Faye's lovely "I'll See You in My Dreams," originally included in a New York supper club sequence, ended on the cutting room floor. "Avalon" and "I'm Always Chasing Rainbows" suffered a similar fate, but ROSE remains one of the most musical of all Faye films.

With the release of this film, an era ended in the film capitol. Jolson, who had brought talking and singing to the screen and then reigned supreme for a decade, played only one more screen role in *Swanee River*. It was a sad end to a noble film career, but Jolie had grown difficult and hard to direct.

With Louis Prima singing "I'm Just Wild About Harry."

Alice's trembling lower lip came in for its share of criticism as evidenced by John Hobart's review in the *San Francisco Chronicle* when he said, "Miss Faye continues to mar her excellent singing with all those facial movements, but she does her role acceptably." *Variety* put the blame elsewhere, "Miss Faye is still plenty on the s.a. side, excepting for a few unfortunate camera angles that don't flatter her chin-line. The Sing Sing exit scene where she tearfully promises 'I'll be waiting' after his five-year sentence is unconvincing."

Frank S. Nugent writing in the *New York Times* thought, "Twentieth Century-Fox's latest tour down Melody Lane has come to the Roxy under the blushing title ROSE OF WASHINGTON SQUARE, the Rose being neither Al Jolson nor Tyrone Power (as we had feared), but Alice Faye, who flowers lushly in the cabarets and flounces of the post-war years. Mr. Jolson's singing of 'Mammy,' 'California, Here I Come' and others is something for the memory book. So is Miss Faye's full-mouthed chanting of 'The Vamp,' 'Rose of Washington Square,' 'I'm Just Wild About Harry' and a few others."

Photoplay felt that, "Alice gives a touching performance as the ambitious young star who still clings to her man, come hell or high water."

With Tyrone Power (scene cut from released print.)

Hollywood Cavalcade

A 20th Century-Fox Picture 1939
A Darryl F. Zanuck Production

With Alan Curtis.

CAST:

Molly Adair	ALICE FAYE
Michael Linnett Connors	DON AMECHE
Dave Spingold	J. EDWARD BROMBERG
Nicky Hayden	Alan Curtis
Pete Tinney	Stuart Erwin
Chief of Police	Jed Prouty
Buster Keaton	Himself
Lyle P. Stout	Donald Meek
Claude	George Givot
Keystone Cops	Eddie Collins
	Hank Mann
	Heinie Conklin
	James Finlayson
	Snub Pollard
Chick, assistant director	Chick Chandler
Roberts	Russell Hicks
Willie	Willie Fung
Bartender in western	Ben Turpin
Sheriff in western	Chester Conklin

with:
Robert Lowery, Ben Welden, Paul Stanton, Mary Forbes, Irving Bacon, Marjorie Beebe, Victor Potel, Lee Duncan, Mack Sennett, Al Jolson and Lynn Bari.

CREDITS:

Director	Irving Cummings
Associate Producer	Harry Joe Brown

Silent picture sequences directed by Malcolm St. Clair and supervised by Mr. Mack Sennett.

Screen play	Irving Pascal
Story	Hilary Lynn
	Brown Holmes

Based upon an original idea by Lou Breslow.
Photographed in Technicolor.

Directors of photography	Ernest Palmer, A.S.C.
	Allen M. Davey, A.S.C.
Technicolor director	Natalie Kalmus
Associate	Henry Jaffa
Art direction	Richard Day
	Wiard B. Ihnen
Set direction	Thomas Little
Film editor	Walter Thompson
Costumes	Herschel
Sound	Eugene Grossman
	Roger Heman
Musical direction	Louis Silvers

Released October 13, 1939. Running time 96 minutes.

SYNOPSIS: On a trip to New York in 1913, Mike and Dave attend a stage performance of "The Man Who Came Back." At the start of act four understudy Molly Adair takes over for the ailing star and electrifies the audience with her persuasive histrionics. Mike hurries backstage following the final curtain to offer her a contract to act in pictures, but she refuses. The next morning Mike succeeds by offering her $100 a week.

In Hollywood, Mike directs Molly's screen test and Mr. Stout, head of Globe Pictures, is impressed but dismayed at the salary they must pay their new film actress. Mike, a former prop boy, directs Molly's first picture costarring Buster Keaton, which, by an ironic accident, turns out to be a wild, pie-throwing comedy. Molly is an immediate sensation in the movies — a star.

As the years pass, Mike tries new ideas and story innovations in filming. The result is long lines forming at box offices for Molly's pictures. When Dave comes into an inheritance he hurries west and joins Mike to form a new company with Molly as their top star. Soon Nicky joins the group as leading man. Though Molly's love for Mike has grown he is so busy with new plans that he fails to return her affection.

Molly abruptly marries Nicky before one of their romantic dramas is completed. At the conclusion of the picture's shooting, Mike fires them both and Molly and Nicky embark for Europe on a honeymoon. On their return they sign with Metro as Mike's fortunes decline and his films become merely elaborate, costly failures.

From a silent comedy sequence.

With Alan Curtis and J. Edward Bromberg.

With Don Ameche and J. Edward Bromberg.

In the 1920's, Molly and Nicky are two of Hollywood's greatest film stars recognized even by Mack Sennett who openly praises them at their fifth anniversary party at the Coconut Grove. In the crowd Molly spies Mike with some flashy friends. He is broke and discouraged. Molly asks Dave, now her successful agent-manager, to get Mike as director for her new film, "Common Clay."

Shooting on the picture is nearly finished when Nicky is killed in an auto accident and Molly hospitalized. Jolson's "Jazz Singer" revolutionizes the industry with songs and talking. Roberts urges Mike to complete "Common Clay" with a double as it is a silent and soon won't be salable. Mike refuses, steals the negative from the studio, and when Molly recovers adds a few talking episodes to finish the picture. At the premiere at the Egyptian theatre in Hollywood Roberts agrees with Dave that they have a hit.

Later at Molly's house, she, Mike, and Dave review their past achievements and overlooking the twinkling lights of Hollywood — their town — look forward to a bright future for talking pictures.

NOTES AND REVIEWS: HOLLYWOOD CAVALCADE was Alice Faye's first Technicolor film and remains the best chronicle of silent film making and the emergence of sound in the waning decade of the 1920's. Ameche was her costar for the fourth time, and they were directed by Irving Cummings, one of Alice's favorite directors.

The December issue of *Picture Play* in 1939 thought that "HOLLYWOOD CAVALCADE is doing for the motion picture what ALEXANDER'S RAGTIME BAND did for popular music. Fully as satisfying, amazingly accurate in facts and figures (If Hollywood can't remember its own history, I don't know who should). It's a comedy-drama of a 'silent director' (Don Ameche) who discovers a stage understudy (Alice Faye) and sees her through four periods of flicker progress from slapstick to talkies."

Though audiences loved the picture and it was one of the year's top money makers for 20th Century-Fox, patrons were puzzled that one of Hollywood's foremost musical singing stars uttered not a note in song. The original script, then titled SHOOTING STARS, called for three Faye songs. Why they were cut remains a mystery, and even Miss Faye cannot recall what their titles were. Recently a portion of Alice's number "Whispering" was discovered in negative form at the studio. One can only speculate on the original intent. Was Molly to sing in an early talkie and thus become a great singing sensation as musicals swept into prominence as the decade closed? Or did Fox cut the songs to conform to a running time more suitable to double-billing? Possibly we will never know.

One fact is clear. The first half of the film dealing with Molly's early years in Hollywood is the better portion of the film itself. *Time*'s review affirmed this theory by stating, ". . . its chief distinction lies in the early sequences that recapture the days when the little industry was growing into long pants." The latter half dealing with Mike's fall from grace in the industry undergoes an abrupt switch in emphasis. Why was

With Stuart Erwin and Don Ameche.

With the Michael Linnett Connors' bathing beauties.

Molly sacrificed for the slowed pace of Mike's follies as a slipping director of costly spectacles?

Undeniably the film's greatest moments are the specially filmed silent sequences supervised by Mack Sennett (tinted effectively in sepia tones) and directed with consummate understanding of that earlier medium by Malcolm St. Clair. These portions of the film are original, historically accurate, and riotously funny. The studio obtained Buster Keaton, long out of work and desperate for a chance to reestablish himself in films; he was to heave a custard pie which Alice would receive right on the button. The scene (according to the account by Keaton in his autobiography MY WONDERFUL WORLD OF SLAPSTICK) involving Alice, Buster, and George Givot, the latter as the villain, went well until Givot speeded up a bit of action which necessitated a speedier throw by Keaton of the pie in question. It struck Alice squarely conveying the proper surprise, but the force wasn't

appreciated. After cleaning up and appearing again on the set she chased Buster around the set and out onto the street with a pie she meant to deliver on his impassive poker face.

In addition to Keaton, other silent luminaries such as Ben Turpin and Chester Conklin made brief appearances as well as Eddie Collins, Hank Mann, Heinie Conklin, James Finlayson and Snub Pollard in an original Keystone Kops sequence. Mack Sennett also appeared as himself to deliver the testimonial in the Coconut Grove sequence.

Though little was said at the time of its release, HOLLYWOOD CAVALCADE is the thinly disguised story of Sennett and his screen-star lover, Mabel Normand. *Time* commented openly, "Filmgoers who knew Hollywood when will have no trouble finding several sources for Don Ameche's composite portrait of a great director, Alice Faye's characterization of the Broadway understudy he transforms into America's sweetheart, Alan Curtis as her leading man and husband, and J. Edward Bromberg's sympathetic study of a producer of the old school." If Faye was indeed Mabel Normand it was the second film in a row in which she found herself playing a real-life personality. This time there were no recriminations or law suits; Sennett had a hand in the production and seemed not to mind that Ameche was playing starmaker Sennett, and Miss Normand had been dead for almost a decade when Faye enacted her on screen in 1939.

If the motivations behind the scenes of HOLLYWOOD CAVALCADE were not always clear the critics were perfectly so in their praise of the film and its craftsmen. In the December 1939 issue *Photoplay* admitted, "Technicolor brings a new beauty to Alice Faye, and her acting ability is by far the best she has yet revealed."

Frank S. Nugent, writing in the *N.Y. Times* said, "Miss Faye's ability to take a pie in the face is a hidden talent we couldn't have suspected; we hate to see it buried again."

Variety in their review concluded with the idea that Alice was often better than her material, stating, "Miss Faye brings looks and earnestness to a part that always is on the borderline of incredulity. Ameche is convincing, and J. Edward Bromberg gets the most from a sympathetic character part."

Barricade

A 20th Century-Fox Picture 1939

CAST:

Emmy Jordan	ALICE FAYE
Hank Topping	WARNER BAXTER
Samuel J. Cady	Charles Winninger
Upton Ward	Arthur Treacher
Ling	Keye Luke
Yen	Willie Fung
Mrs. Ward	Doris Lloyd
Mrs. Little	Eily Malyon
Winifred	Joan Carroll
Boris (Russian Consul)	Leonid Snegoff
Col Wai Kang	Philip Ahn
Asst. Sec. of State	Jonathan Hale
Managing Editor	Moroni Olsen
Telegraph Manager	Harry Hayden

CREDITS:

Director	Gregory Ratoff
Producer	Darryl F. Zanuck
Story and screen play	Granville Walker
Editor	Jack Dennis
Photographer	Karl Freund, A.S.C.
Art directors	Bernard Herzbrun
	Haldane Douglas
Set decoration	Thomas Little
Costumes	Royer
Sound	George Leverett
	Roger Heman
Music	David Buttolph
Associate Producer	Edward Kaufman

Released December 8, 1939. Running time 71 minutes.

Song: "There'll Be Other Nights" by Lew Brown and Lew Pollack. (Cut from release print.)

SYNOPSIS: On a crowded train bound for Shanghai, Emmy Jordan, posing as a Russian, meets Hank Topping, an American newspaper man well in his cups. When bandits tear up the tracks ahead, and the train is forced to return to the interior, Emmy leaves the train and seeks refuge in the American consulate of Pangchow run by the kindly Mr. Cady.

Hank follows her, and during dinner that evening Cady gets word that a Chinese officer will take them to a nearby rail center. Hank, however, recognizes the officer as a marked man, and to prevent Emmy going with him, he locks her in a closet. Moments later they watch as the officer's car is attacked by bandits, and he is killed.

Singing "There'll Be Other Nights"
(cut from released print.)

The following day Cady drives into the nearby town to rescue American missionaries trapped there. Emmy tells Hank her real name and admits that she burned her passport, but she does not tell him why. Cady returns with the missionaries. They have been fired upon by the bandits, and Cady quickly arms the group preparing them for the worst.

Emmy realizes she is falling in love with Hank, and when he writes a thrilling news story about Cady, she insists he wire the story to his news service. Together they enter the town, where in a moment of near panic Emmy admits that she killed a man. They succeed in sending most of the message. Then Hank is forced to shoot the son of the bandit chieftain so they can escape.

Emmy and Hank are pursued through burning wheat fields to the consulate, and the siege of the tiny compound begins. Finally, their ammunition almost gone, the members of the small fortress take refuge in the cellar. Just when it looks as though the bandits will break through the trap door and slaughter the terrified Americans, the Chinese nationalist army arrives, and the bandits are captured. Mr. Cady is recalled to Washington by the President, and Hank and Emmy will marry after clearing her name of the murder charge.

With Warner Baxter (a scene cut from the released print.)

With Warner Baxter.

With Willie Fung and Warner Baxter.

NOTES AND REVIEWS: ''BARRICADE was launched as an A but winds up as a B release that will have to groove generally in the supporting spots,'' said *Variety* when the film was released in December of 1939.

That it ever reached release at all is a minor miracle in view of the fact that it was never finished. Cast and crew never really believed in the weak story line, and after shooting had been in progress for some weeks in 1938, a halt was called, and the unfinished footage cooled its heels on the shelf for a year. A mandarin's palace with a dress ball was called for in the original script, and Miss Faye, a cafe singer, was supposed to be the only witness to the mandarin's murder. When the murderer threatened her, Emmy killed him and fled. The released print actually commenced at this point though scattered scenes had been filmed.

Two supporting names, J. Edward Bromberg and Joseph Schildkraut, were entirely edited from the footage. Arthur Treacher, given fourth billing, had only three lines and appeared in but two sequences. Due to the growing box office draw of the Faye name, the studio decided to patch together the footage and release it hoping to recoup the investment. Editor Dennis did a commendable job, for though it does contain holes in the story, and Alice's hair styles are seen to change abruptly in the middle of a conversation, what results is an often tense, exciting film. Begun as THE GIRL FROM BROOKLYN, the title seemed unsuited to a Chinese setting, so it became BY DAWN'S EARLY LIGHT. This was thought to be confusing and might suggest a story involving the writing of "The Star Spangled Banner." WHITE LADY OF THE ORIENT was the most workable and original title, and stills were actually printed with that title. Released as BARRICADE, the film not only earned back its investment but turned a modest profit as well. It is a film Alice prefers to forget entirely, but in the early days of television broadcasting it was one of the most frequently televised Faye features.

It does possess some fascinating sets and the photography of Karl Freund, who won an Oscar in 1937 for THE GOOD EARTH, was exceptional.

With Warner Baxter and Charles Winninger.

Frank S. Nugent strove for playful humor in his *New York Times* review. "It's a flimsy BAR-RICADE Twentieth Century-Fox raised at the Roxy yesterday. . . . We thought, for example, that the murder Alice Faye committed in a cafe in Kalgan, Northern China, before the film began was one of the most stirring sequences we have not seen this year. We knew this must be so because, later, Miss Faye became hysterical at the mere mention of it and shuddered at the sight of a gun. We knew it, too, because Warner Baxter, who plays the cynical free-lance corre-

spondent, took her in his arms, looked deep in her eyes and murmured, 'Whoever it was you killed, I'm sure he had it coming to him.' It must have been a beautiful murder."

Alice recorded and filmed one song for this production entitled "There'll Be Other Nights." It was a bright, breezy number delivered at the Continental Hotel in Kalgan while enthralled patrons looked on including an evil-appearing Joseph Schildkraut. Because the early sequences had not been filmed, it could not be used and was scrapped.

SUPER STAR

1940·1945

As the decade of the turbulent forties began, Alice Faye stood at the peak of a most successful career. She was beloved by movie audiences everywhere, and her name in lights a foot high at the Roxy in New York or in small letters on the marquee of the Princess Theatre in Emonds, Washington, meant capacity business.

To loyal film fans she seemed the epitome of glamour, sophistication, and self-assurance. If former doubts and uncertainties about her ability or worth as a star still troubled her, it was not apparent. She was controlled and dignified. Perhaps lady-like is old-fashioned by today's standards, but Alice Faye was never anything but a lady down to her lovely manicured fingertips.

The mischievious twinkle in the eyes, the playful smile trailing off into a soul-searching sadness, and the trembling mouth when she sang were still very much in evidence. Now the gowns were luxurious and elegantly chic, the makeup soft and smartly feminine, but the old Faye stance could still be seen in every picture.

She still sailed off for that big break in London in TIN PAN ALLEY and HELLO, FRISCO, HELLO or better still sought romance in the sunny climes of RIO and HAVANA. She was happily competent in comedy such as the affable barmaid in LITTLE OLD NEW YORK, believable as the glamorous LILLIAN RUSSELL, and at home before a radio mike in THE GREAT AMERICAN BROADCAST or FOUR JILLS IN A JEEP. For contrast there was the splashy color in THE GANG'S ALL HERE to compete with her emotional intensity in FALLEN ANGEL.

But Faye was never cast in a mold. Most stars continued to plug along in roles for years with diminishing returns until they were dropped or replaced by others. Many saw Alice as a second Garbo—quitting while she was ahead. Quit she did when the demand by both studio and public for additional appearances was at its height.

Many questioned the wisdom of such a move. But right or wrong, it was the lady's choice, and maybe it's better just that way. Who was it that said, "Always leave them wanting more?"

Little Old New York

A 20th Century-Fox Picture 1940
A Darryl F. Zanuck Production

CAST:

Pat O'Day	ALICE FAYE
Charles Browne	FRED MacMURRAY
Robert Fulton	RICHARD GREENE
Harriett Livingston	Brenda Joyce
Commodore	Andy Devine
Chancellor Livingston	Henry Stephenson
Noah	Ben Carter
Regan	Ward Bond
Tavern Keeper	Fritz Feld
Willie Stout	Clarence Hummel Wilson
Nicholas Roosevelt	Robert Middlemass
John Jacob Astor	Roger Imhof
Washington Irving	Theodore Von Eltz
Mrs. Brevoort	Virginia Brissac

with

Jody Gilbert, Arthur Aylesworth, Stanley Andrews, O. G. Hendrian, Harry Tyler, Victor Kilian, Paul Sutton, Tyler Brooke, Herbert Ashley, Herbert Heywood.

CREDITS:

Director	Henry King
Producer	Darryl F. Zanuck
Associate Producer	Raymond Griffith
Screenplay	Harry Tugend
Story	John Balderson
Editor	Barbara McLean
Photography	Leon Shamroy A.S.C.
Music	Alfred Newman
Art direction	Richard Day
	Rudolph Sternad
Special effects	Fred Sersen
Set decoration	Thomas Little
Marine art direction	James Havens
Costumes	Royer
Sound	Alfred Bruzlin
	Roger Heman

SONG: "Who Is the Beau of the Belle of New York" by Mack Gordon.

Released February 9, 1940. Running time 100 minutes.

OPENING LEGEND: "New York 1807. The greatest harbor in the New World. Behind a forest of masts rose a turbulent city . . . a melting pot of adventurers from every land."

SYNOPSIS: Arriving in New York following his latest experiments on the Seine, Robert Fulton takes lodgings in the Bull's Head Tavern run by Pat O'Day, an attractive, good-natured young woman with an eye for business. Fulton pays a call at the home of the Chancellor

With Fred MacMurray, Andy Devine and Richard Greene.

With Henry Stephenson, Richard Greene and Brenda Joyce.

hoping for continued financial support to build his steamboat. There he meets Harriett, the Chancellor's niece, and becomes enamored of her. After a minor setback Pat's lover, Charlie Browne, undertakes the construction of Fulton's *Clermont*. Late one night a gang of waterfront ruffians led by the villainous Regan, fearful that the steamboat will put them out of work, marches on the shipyard and burns the unfinished ship. When Livingston withdraws further support, Pat and her friends undertake the job. Pat buys kegs of rum on credit from Willie Stout and sells them for less money to her competitors, turning over the cash to Fulton whom she fancies is in love with her. Charlie, angered by

her interest in Fulton, threatens to walk out, but Pat begs him to finish work on the ship. He agrees, but relations between him and Fulton become strained. After President Jefferson signs the embargo against British manufactured material entering the country, Charlie and Fulton, with the aid of the Commodore, outwit Regan and the harbor patrol, and under cover of darkness and a heavy fog, bring the engine ashore from a British freighter. The great day arrives, and the harbor is crowded as "Fulton's Folly" sails slowly up the Hudson. Pat, realizing at last that Fulton loves Harriet, accepts the advances of Charlie, and the age of steam is a reality.

NOTES AND REVIEWS: LITTLE OLD NEW YORK had been a silent screen vehicle for Marion Davies in 1923 and a play by Rida Johnson Young. In the original screen treatment Fulton and the steamboat had only been a minor episode, but in the Fox version it was the mainstay of the story. The film marked Alice Faye's emergence into straight comedy which she handled with consummate skill prompting the *New York Times* to state: "LITTLE OLD NEW YORK is a diverting screen show . . . Miss Faye is a good comedienne and realized all comic possibilities." For the third film in a row Alice did not sing a number except to join in the chorus of "Who Is the Beau of the Belle of New York" a number sung by Tyler Brooke in the rathskeller sequence. The production was expensively mounted with a huge harbor set constructed on the studio back lot with full-scale sailing ships. *Variety* remarked, "Henry King's direction is paced very slowly, but this may also perhaps be attributed to Harry Tugend's sprawling screenplay. On the production end, however, the film got and shows expensive mounting." But the film was Miss Faye's from the start as Frank S. Nugent stated in his review, "Miss Faye is a tavern wench with delusions of grandeur and a yen for a bustle. She begins to realize the comic possibilities latent in a pair of blue eyes of high batting average and a mouth that was never meant for Lady Macbeth."
LITTLE OLD NEW YORK was the third and final Faye film directed by Henry King, it also marked the only time she starred with Fred MacMurray or Richard Greene and the third time she was supported by Andy Devine.

*With Ben Carter,
Clarence Hummel Wilson
and Richard Greene.*

With Ward Bond and O.G. Hendrian.

With Theodore Von Eltz, Virginia Brissac and Robert Middlemass.

With Fred MacMurray.

129

Lillian Russell
A 20th Century-Fox Picture 1940
A Darryl F. Zanuck Production

CAST:

Lillian Russell .... ALICE FAYE
Edward Solomon .... DON AMECHE
Alexander Moore .... HENRY FONDA
Diamond Jim Brady .... EDWARD ARNOLD
Jesse Lewisohn .... Warren William
Tony Pastor .... Leo Carrillo
Grandma Leonard .... Helen Westley
Cynthia Leonard .... Dorothy Peterson
Charles Leonard .... Ernest Truex
Edna McCauley .... Lynn Bari
William Gilbert .... Nigel Bruce
Arthur Sullivan .... Claude Allister
Weber and Fields .... Joe Weber &
　　　　　　　　　　　　　　Lew Fields
Marie .... Una O'Connor
Eddie Foy, Sr. .... Eddie Foy, Jr.
Leopold Damrosch .... Joseph Cawthorn
President Cleveland .... William B. Davidson
with:
Cecil Cunningham, Hal K. Dawson, Robert Emmett Keane, Frank Darien, Irving Bacon, William Haade, and Harry Hayden.

CREDITS:

Producer .... Darryl F. Zanuck
Associate producer .... Gene Markey
Director .... Irving Cummings
Screen play .... William Anthony McGuire
Cameraman .... Leon Shamroy, A.S.C.
Dances .... Seymour Felix
Set decoration .... Thomas Little
Art direction .... Richard Day
　　　　　　　　　　　　　Joseph C. Wright
Film editor .... Walter Thompson
Costumes .... Travis Banton
Sound .... Arthur von Kirbach
　　　　　　　　　　　　　　Roger Heman
Musical direction .... Alfred Newman

Released May 24, 1940. Running time 127 minutes.

SONGS: "Adored One" by Mack Gordon and Alfred Newman, "Blue Love Bird" by Gus Kahn and Bronislau Kaper, "Waltz Is King" by Mack Gordon and Charles Henderson, "Back in the Days of Old Broadway" by Charles Henderson and Alfred Newman.

(Old standards): "Ma Blushin' Rosie" (My Posie Sweet) by John Stromberg and Edgar Smith; "After the Ball" by Charles K. Harris; "Come Down Ma' Evenin' Star" by John Stromberg and Robert B. Smith, "Comin' Thro' the Rye" (Scotch traditional melody) Robert Burns. "He Goes to Church on Sunday" E. Ray Goetz, Vincent Bryan.

As Lillian (following her London triumph.)

SYNOPSIS: Charlie Leonard's Clinton, Iowa, household is filled with girls, so he hopes his last child will be a boy. At her birth Charlie agrees that his youngest daughter has a powerful voice. Following the Civil War the family moves to New York where Helen, encouraged by Grandma Leonard, is accepted as a pupil by the renowned Leopold Damrosch who tells her she has a pleasing voice though one not suitable for grand opera, her original goal. Returning home, Helen and her grandmother are rescued by a darkly handsome young man who stops their runaway horses frightened by a suffragette band. Grandma Leonard does not approve of her daughter-in-law's political aspirations and is not surprised when Cynthia Leonard polls only a handful of votes in her bid for mayor of New York.

While "playing theatre" in the back yard for her father, Helen's singing is overheard by Tony Pastor who immediately hires her for his theatre. He renames her Lillian Russell and bills her as "The Great English Ballad Singer." Lillian is

With Una O'Connor.

With Henry Fonda.

*Most of the period carriages and much
of the furnishings including a whole room in the
New York home of the Leonards was auctioned
off by the firm of Sotheby-Parke-Bernet
in February 1971.

unable to forget the brave young man who saved her life, but as she becomes the toast of New York Alexander Moore fades out of her life.

Now a famous star, Lillian has shows written especially for her; corsets, cigars, and roses are named for her, and her suitors, in addition to millionaire Diamond Jim Brady, include Jesse Lewisohn and a brooding young musician, Edward Solomon. Shortly after making history by singing over the long-distance telephone for President Cleveland, Lillian marries "Teddy" Solomon and shortly afterwards departs for London where Gilbert and Sullivan are writing an operetta especially for her.

It is here that Alexander Moore finds her and contracts for a series of articles based upon her successful life for his American newspaper. Lillian, now the mother of a baby girl, is heartbroken when her husband dies suddenly while composing music for a show to star her. The interviews are cancelled and Moore again fades from her life. Before sailing for home with her maid, Marie, Lillian makes a triumphant appearance singing one of Teddy's songs.

Back in America the legend grows with the years as Lillian becomes the greatest stage attraction of the century, appearing with such personalities as Eddie Foy and Weber and Fields. Now the owner of his own paper, Moore comes backstage after the opening of a new show and he and Lillian are happily reunited.

NOTES AND REVIEWS: One of the year's most costly productions, LILLIAN RUSSELL was stunningly produced. Never had Alice Faye been so beautifully gowned, so superbly coiffured, nor been featured in such stunningly photographed closeups. The sets and furnishings* were historically accurate down to the smallest degree. It remains a mystery why the whole production was not filmed in Technicolor, or why HOLLYWOOD CAVALCADE the previous year had been when the story essentially did not warrant it. It would undoubtedly have added to the box-office return had the vivid hues of the Fox technicians been so employed.

It was the longest film of Faye's career and the only one to run over two hours. Once again Alice was directed by the meticulous Irving Cummings and costarred for the fifth time with Don Ameche. Alice recently stated that she felt

LILLIAN RUSSELL was her most difficult screen assignment in that the title role was so completely different personality-wise from her own life and experience. It was Alice's only screen appearance with Henry Fonda. Fonda, never happy at Fox except for his THE GRAPES OF WRATH role, felt this was one of his worst film appearances and has little to say in its favor.

Critics for the most part disliked the film, but it was vastly popular with audiences and made a great deal of money. *Variety* chided the production as, "A story which is scarcely more than a broad burlesque of a career that was rich in sentiment and background. Lillian Russell for more than a generation was one of America's greatest women personalities, on and off, and she left a deep imprint on national manners and customs. Her cinematic biography is disappointing." The same review admitted, "Miss Faye in the title part wears the costumes of the period with graceful ease, and she does the song hits of

With Helen Westley and Joseph Cawthorn.

"Ma' Blushin' Rosie" production number (at Tony Pastor's in New York.)

With Edward Arnold.

long ago pleasantly." Indicating that the period of the story wasn't all it might be, the review concluded in a humorous vein, "Maybe the film is right, after all; perhaps the '90's weren't so gay."

Bosley Crowther in his *New York Times* article struck a humorous note as well by claiming, "Miss Russell is said to have been a rather poor actress, and Miss Faye — even granting the thinness of her material — does not violate that reputation. Throughout she seems little more than a pampered and alarmingly virtuous family girl."

Not all critics were unkind, however. *Photoplay* in August felt that, "In a difficult role Alice does a really splendid job, even achieving a special kind of dignity." *Picture Show* on September 21st stated simply, "Alice Faye gives a most charming performance and sings in her usual manner."

Part of the trouble obviously lay in the script of William Anthony McGuire which began auspiciously but which ended up rather leaden. McGuire wisely eliminated two of Lillian's four husbands, but allowed the situations to drag by not providing enough of a showcase for the Faye voice. One number, a dreary "Last Rose of Summer" was cut before the film's release. However, the overall pace was admittedly slow. Ameche's role of Solomon presented him merely as a snarling, petulant bore which any actor would have had difficulty overcoming.

Edward Arnold was letter perfect as Diamond Jim. It was his second time in the part, having played the title role in DIAMOND JIM five years before for Universal. Helen Westly as Grandma had one of the showcase roles of her film career. Weber and Fields were brought out of retirement to play themselves, a happy stroke of casting as their work would otherwise be remembered only on scratchy, primitive recordings. The bickerings of Gilbert and Sullivan were briefly chronicled by Claude Allister and Nigel Bruce for telling effect perfectly in keeping with their real lives, but Diane Fisher as Lillian's daughter, a mercifully brief part, is a precious child in the worst tradition of screen moppets all syrupy sweetness from her toes to her cunning pouting lips.

Singing "Blue Lovebird."

Tin Pan Alley

A 20th Century-Fox Picture 1940

Doing "The Sheik of Araby" number with Billy Gilbert and Betty Grable.

CAST:

Katie Blane	ALICE FAYE
Lily Blane	BETTY GRABLE
Harry Calhoun	JACK OAKIE
Skeets Harrigan	JOHN PAYNE
Casey	Allen Jenkins
Nora Bayes	Esther Ralston
Reggie Carstair	John Loder
Joe Codd	Elisha Cook, Jr.
Harvey Raymond	Fred Keating
Sheik	Billy Gilbert
Lord Stanley	Lionel Pape

with:
Ben Carter, Lillian Porter, Tyler Brooke, Hal K. Dawson, William B. Davidson, Billy Bevan, Dewey Robinson, Robert Emmett Keane, John Sheehan, George Watts.
Specialties:
Nicholas Brothers, Princess Vanessa Ammon, Brian Sisters, and Roberts Brothers.

CREDITS:

Director	Walter Lang
Screenplay	Robert Ellis
	Helen Logan
Musical director	Alfred Newman
Dances	Seymour Felix
Photography	Leon Shamroy, A.S.C.
Art directors	Richard Day
	Joseph C. Wright
Set decoration	Thomas Little
Editor	Walter Thompson
Costumes	Travis Banton
Sound	Eugene Grossman
	Roger Heman
Associate producer	Kenneth MacGowan

Released November 29, 1940. Running time 92 minutes.

SONGS: (New) "You Say the Sweetest Things, Baby" by Mack Gordon and Harry Warren. (Old) "America, I Love You" by Edgard Leslie and Archie Gottler. "Goodbye, Broadway, Hello, France," by Francis Reisner, Benny Davis and Billy Baskette. "K-K-K-Katy" by Geoffrey O'Hara. "Moonlight Bay" by Edward Madden and Percy Wenrich. "Honeysuckle Rose" by Andy Razof and Thomas Waller. "The Sheik of Araby" by Harry B. Smith, Francis Wheeler, and Ted Snyder.

SYNOPSIS: Threatened with eviction for non-payment of rent, Harry and Skeets try to get a song they've been kicking around plugged by a name act. They hit upon the Blane sisters who introduce the number, but almost get fired for their unorthodox initiative. That evening while Katie is dining with the boys they hear an interesting song being played by its composer, Joe Codd. They make a deal with Joe, using Katie's money, and the song becomes a sensation. When Lily goes into a new show, Katie gives up the stage, goes to work for Harrigan and Calhoun's "The House That Hits Built." Business booms, new offices are acquired, and all goes well with Katie, the name who sells the latest tunes. Skeets obtains a new song destined, he feels, to be their biggest hit. Katie is to introduce it at the NVA benefit and obtains a new wardrobe for the occasion, but Skeets, unable to say no to a big-name performer, gives the number to Nora Bayes. Heartsick at Skeets' indifference, Katie joins Lily in London where the girls become the toast of the musical stage. Fortune turns for Skeets and Harry when Skeets refuses another of Joe's songs, a war tune Skeets feels will not go over because there isn't going to be a war. War is declared, their business is dead without Katie, so the boys enlist in the army and are sent to England. Unable to get a pass, they go AWOL to London to catch the final performance of Katie and Lily in their latest show. All four are reunited at the dock that night where doughboys are embarking for the front. While clowning, Harry falls into the harbor, and while calling goodbye to Katie the lyrics for "K-K-K-Katy" are born — the perfect lyrics for the song which would never jell before. At the war's end Katie is reunited with Skeets as the troops march triumphantly down Fifth Avenue in New York.

NOTES AND REVIEWS: TIN PAN ALLEY was originally intended as a vehicle for Faye, Tyrone Power and Don Ameche, the studio reasoning that another

With John Payne.

137

ALEXANDER'S RAGTIME BAND cast would spell box-office gold. Casting assignments necessitated shifts, Oakie and Payne were brought in, and a part written for Betty Grable who had just clicked in DOWN ARGENTINE WAY. The latter picture was slated for Alice but given to Betty when the former underwent an operation for appendicitis.

The net result was a happy coincidence of fast-paced comedy, skillful blending of old and new songs, and one of the most musical Faye films since BAND two years before. "In addition to infectious and solid entertainment factors," said *Variety*, " 'Tin Pan Alley' unfolds at a consistently fast clip throughout and is provided with top A production mounting. Photography by Leon Shamroy is of highest standard."

The big "Sheik of Araby" production number ran into censorship problems with the Hays office for showing too much of the chorus girls' torsos and was judiciously trimmed. "Capitalizing on their more obvious assets, the film sets Alice and Betty wriggling and crooning in cellophane hula skirts and harem costumes," carped a critic in *Time*.

With John Payne, Jack Oakie and Allen Jenkins.

This was John Payne's first costarring assignment with Alice. They were a well-balanced team and starred together in three additional pictures. Only Don Ameche with six starring assignments with Alice to his credit appeared more often than Payne in Faye films. The Academy of Motion Picture Arts and Sciences awarded Alfred Newman an Oscar for "best score" for 1940 for his outstanding work in TIN PAN ALLEY.

20th Century-Fox was never noted for their accurate period costume films, but ALLEY was an exception, and the hobble skirts of pre-World War I vintage were beautifully executed by Travis Banton, and the hats and furs worn by Faye and Grable were authentic and accurate, giving a sense of the times which would surely have garnered an Oscar nomination for Banton except that costume design awards were not given by the Academy until 1948.

With John Payne.

One musical number entitled "Get Out and Get Under" was cut before release. It involved Alice, Betty and Oakie on an outing in a vintage flivver. The recorded number survives today as well as several stills of this sequence.

*The "Get Out and Get Under" number
with Betty Grable and Jack Oakie (cut from released print.)*

*With Jack Oakie,
Betty Grable and John Payne.*

That Night in Rio

A 20th Century-Fox Picture 1941

CAST:

Baroness Cecilia Duarte .... ALICE FAYE
Larry Martin)
Baron Duarte) .... DON AMECHE
Carmen .... CARMEN MIRANDA
Penna .... S. Z. Sakall
Machado .... J. Carrol Naish
Salles .... Curt Bois
Pierre .... Leonid Kinskey
Pedro .... Frank Puglia
Luiza .... Lillian Porter
Inez .... Maria Montez
Ambassador .... Georges Renavent
Alfonso .... Edward Conrad
Pereira .... Fortunio Bonanova
Specialty Trio .... Flores Brothers
&
The Banda da Lua ...... Carmen Miranda's Orchestra

CREDITS:

Director .... Irving Cummings
Associate Producer .... Fred Kohlmar
Screen play .... George Seaton, Bess Meredyth,
Hal Long
Additional dialogue .... Samuel Hoffenstein
Based on a play by ... Rudolph Lothar and Hans Adler
Adapted by .... Jessie Ernst
Dances staged by .... Hermes Pan
Directors of photography ..... Leon Shamroy, A.S.C.,
Ray Rennahan, A.S.C.
Technicolor director .... Natalie Kalmus
Associate .... Morgan Padelford
Musical director .... Alfred Newman
Art directors .... Richard Day
Joseph C. Wright
Set decorations .... Thomas Little
Film editor .... Walter Thompson
Costumes .... Travis Banton
Sound .... W. D. Flick, Roger Heman

Released April 11, 1941. Running time 90 minutes.

SONGS: "I'yi, Yi, Yi, Yi" (I Like You Very Much); "Chica, Chica, Boom, Chic"; "Boa Noite" (Good Night); "They Met in Rio"; "The Baron Is in Conference" by Mack Gordon and Harry Warren.

SYNOPSIS: Accompanied by her debonair, man-about-town husband, the lovely Baroness Duarte and party arrive at the lush Casino Samba to see the headline attrac-

tion, Larry Martin, a dead ringer for the Baron, do his famed impersonation of Duarte. They find the act amazingly realistic, and the Baron assures Pereira, the manager, that they are not offended. Backstage, the Baron runs into an old flame, Inez. Carmen, mistaking the Baron for

With J. Carrol Naish and Don Ameche.

Larry, at first berates him and then apologizes when she learns the truth. He invites her to a party he is giving the following evening for the ambassador, but she declines.

Later that evening Larry meets the Baroness and is attracted by her beauty and lovely singing. She asks him to impersonate the Baron for her so she can examine his skill close at hand and he complies. The Baron meanwhile receives news that his airline is in danger because an important contract is not being renewed. Confident that it would be, the Baron speculated earlier and purchased fifty-one percent of the stock using some of the bank's money. Sure that the news will not be made public for forty-eight

hours, the Baron leaves town to try and raise the needed cash.

Penna and Salles hire Larry to front for the Baron at the stock exchange to calm the suspicious Machado, but Larry complicates matters by inadvertently buying the additional forty-nine percent of the airline stock. At the party for the ambassador that evening Larry is still impersonating the Baron, though Cecilia has been informed of the substitution.

When Carmen learns that Larry is at the Baron's home she throws herself into an explosive rage wrecking his dressing room and hastily decides to join the party. Larry and Carmen quarrel in the library, but when Cecilia enters,

With Leonid Kinskey, Curt Bois, Don Ameche and S.Z. Sakall.

Larry tells her that Carmen has arrived to sing for the guests.

Machado finally corners Larry in the library to discuss business. Fearful that they will be overheard he converses in French which Larry does not understand. Suddenly the Baron returns from an unsuccessful attempt to raise the necessary twenty million and learns that his wife has been flirting with Larry. Pledging the servants to secrecy he gets rid of Larry and makes violent love to his wife who is sure that Larry is living his part too well.

The next morning Cecilia is told that the Baron's plane just landed. Fearing that she has been unfaithful to her husband she learns the truth from Larry.

Meanwhile at the office the Baron is conferring with his associates when Machado enters and smilingly presents him with a check for thirty-two million, his payment for the Baron's airline, the result of his conversation with Larry the evening before. His reputation saved and his fortune intact, the Baron departs for home.

Cecilia once more engages Larry to make love to her so that her husband will be jealous and mend his romantic meanderings, but the Baron turns the tables on her. Thus at the fadeout Larry and Carmen are reunited for a tempestuous future, and the Baron and Baroness face a happy future together.

With Don Ameche and Carmen Miranda.

With Don Ameche and Leonid Kinskey.

Alice Faye's twenty-sixth film began life with the working title of THE ROAD TO RIO, but Paramount had begun its successful series of ROAD pictures the previous year and owned rights to that title. Seven years later Bing, Bob and Dottie traveled the ROAD TO RIO as that series swung into its final stages. THAT NIGHT IN RIO was a remake (a common practice at Fox) of the very successful 1935 FOLIES BERGERE with Maurice Chevalier in the Ameche role, Ann Sothern in the part played by Miranda and Merle Oberon enacting the part done here by Faye. The two films follow a duplicate story line with few changes, and often the dialogue of the latter is an exact carbon copy of the former. FOLIES was historic from the standpoint of the first dance direction Oscar for Dave Gould for his inventive "Straw Hat" production number which in turn followed the Busby Berkeley school of overhead shooting. Oscars for dance direction were not given after 1937.

Dressed up in the outstanding Fox brand of Technicolor which was second to none in Hollywood, the film was a lush, snappy production with some surprisingly risque dialogue and double-entendres frowned upon by the strict code then rigidly in force. One scene requiring Ameche to make love to Faye while the latter thinks he is Larry Martin was excised for American viewing but retained for English and European audiences.

The sets and costumes were especially lavish and elegant, but nothing about the production gave evidence of a South American setting. Rio could just as easily have been Buenos Aires, Mexico City or Santiago, for not one location shot or montage sequence was employed to set the tone for the tropical Rio metropolis. Audiences seemed not to mind, and the film was a financial bonanza.

RIO was Faye's second Technicolor film. She never looked more lovely and audiences still fondly recall her first entrance wearing the pale blue evening gown with its hood trimmed in sumptuous fur. Though she received top, star billing, Alice took a back seat to Ameche in a dual role, his footage far surpassing hers. THAT NIGHT IN RIO remains at this writing Ameche's personal favorite of all his film roles. RIO was to

The "Chica, Chica, Boom, Chic" opening production number.

be the final screen teaming of Faye and Ameche — their sixth.

The popularity of Carmen Miranda was rapidly rising following her U.S. film debut the year before in DOWN ARGENTINE WAY. In THAT NIGHT IN RIO she played her first screen role (she had been herself in the previous film) setting a pattern of rapid-fire dialogue punctuated by her unique brand of fractured English. Film audiences loved her brand of humor throughout the years of World War II, but she made only twelve additional films before her untimely death in 1955 at the age of forty-one.

The Gordon-Warren score for THAT NIGHT IN RIO was breezy and bright, but only "Chica, Chica, Boom, Chic" seemed to fall within the hit classification, and that was due in no small measure to the opening production number spectacularly choreographed by Hermes Pan.

For those who came away puzzled that Fox's biggest singing star was given but two brief choruses to sing let it be noted for the record that Alice and Ameche recorded and filmed "Chica, Chica, Boom Chic" as a song-dance number. For some reason it was not used in the release prints and is gathering dust in the studio's vaults."

Bosley Crowther writing in the *New York Times* on March 10th stated, "There is also Miss Faye, slightly torpid, but still able to fill out a sensational gown or a throaty song like 'They Met in Rio' . . . and there are enough gorgeous girls in stunning dresses to knock the eyes out of a strict misogynist."

Photoplay for June 1941 was more colorfully sassy by saying, "Miranda is a riot. Ameche is peachy (he'll kill us for that), Faye too luscious and the whole doggone thing a wow."

The British publication *Picture Show* declared, "This is a first-rate musical — one of the best of its kind ever put on the screen. To begin with it has a good story — on the musical side the picture is equally strong."

145

The Great American Broadcast

A 20th Century-Fox Picture 1941

CAST:

Vicki Adams .... ALICE FAYE
Chuck Hadley .... JACK OAKIE
Rix Martin .... JOHN PAYNE
Bruce Chadwick .... Cesar Romero
Specialty .... Four Ink Spots
Singer .... James Newill
Specialties .... Nicholas Brothers
                                  Wiere Brothers
Secretary .... Mary Beth Hughes
Madame Rinaldi .... Eula Morgan
Foreman .... William Pawley
Justice of the Peace .... Lucien Littlefield
Conductor .... Edward Conrad
Announcers .... Gary Breckner
                                  Mike Frankovich
                                  John Hiestand
Jimmy .... Eddie Acuff
Jennie .... Mildred Gover
Brakeman .... Syd Saylor
Headwaiter .... Eddie Kane
Mr. Porter .... William Halligan
Counter Man .... Frank Orth
Doorman .... Herbert Heywood

CREDITS:

Director .... Archie Mayo
Associate producer .... Kenneth MacGowan
Original screen play .... Don Ettlinger, Edwin Blum,
                          Robert Ellis, Helen Logan
Musical director .... Alfred Newman
Directors of photography ...... Leon Shamroy A.S.C.
                                Peverell Marley A.S.C.
Art direction .... Richard Day
                                  Albert Hogsett
Set decorations .... Thomas Little
Film editor .... Robert Simpson
Costumes .... Travis Banton
Sound .... Joseph E. Aiken
                                  Roger Heman

Released May 9, 1941. Running time 90 minutes.

SONGS: "I've Got a Bone to Pick with You," "I Take to You," "It's All in a Lifetime," "Long Ago Last Night," "Where You Are" and "The Great American Broadcast" by Mack Gordon and Harry Warren. "Alabamy Bound" by Buddy DeSylva, Bud Green, and Ray Henderson. "Give My Regards to Broadway" by George M. Cohan and "If I Didn't Care" by Jack Lawrence.

With John Payne and Jack Oakie.

SYNOPSIS: Rix Martin is a young man with ideas, financed by World War I comrade Bruce Chadwick. The latest venture, an air service and airport, has failed like all the others. Rix encounters Chuck and learns about the possibilities of sending messages and music through the air — a new concept — radio. He is enthusiastic about the new medium especially after meeting Chuck's girl Vicki, a singer in a speakeasy.

Their initial venture, an opera broadcast from the roof of a Jersey warehouse during an electrical storm, is hardly a success. However, Rix is sure radio can be a success if they broadcast an event of great public interest. Their chance comes with the Willard-Dempsey title bout in

With John Payne and Jack Oakie.

Toledo in 1919. Rix and Chuck set up their equipment in a railroad station and Vicki joins Rix at ringside during the fight. The result is an overwhelming success for radio and a personal triumph as Vicki and Rix realize their love for each other. Rix and Chuck part company, but radio broadcasting has caught on and stations open across the country. Vicki, now married to Rix, works in their small station, a setup unable to compete with the larger broadcasting studios.

Needing money to expand and modernize their equipment, Rix applies for a bank loan. Unknown to him Vickie lunches with Bruce who agrees to put up the money needed for their station. When Rix hears that Bruce is behind the venture he walks out on Vickie. She ultimately goes to work for New York's biggest broadcast-

ing station, WAB, owned and operated by Chuck and Bruce.

The years pass and Vickie becomes the number one vocalist on radio, but Rix has disappeared. Chuck realizes that Vickie never really loved him, but is dismayed when she admits she is going to Reno to divorce Rix and marry Bruce. In desperation, realizing she still loves Rix, Chuck proposes a nationwide hookup, a "Great American Broadcast," another scheme Rix suggested years before. Chuck claims in print that the idea is original with him, knowing this will bring Rix back if anything will. As the musical variety program is beamed across the nation Rix appears, is reunited with Vickie, and big-time coast-to-coast radio broadcasting is a success.

NOTES AND REVIEWS: For film buffs recounting Faye films from memory THE GREAT AMERICAN BROADCAST is often overlooked or forgotten. This is an injustice, for of the five films in which Alice was directly connected with radio broadcasting it is the best in all categories. It possesses the best script, direction, and contained some of the best musical numbers written for the screen by the team of Gordon and Warren. It was, however, the final "story for radio" of Faye's career and the only time she was directed by Archie Mayo. Again her costars of John Payne and Jack Oakie proved box office, a team destined for one more Faye venture two years later.

The opening screen credits with vignettes by radio personalities Jack Benny, Kate Smith, Eddie Cantor, Rudy Vallee and Walter Winchell added the proper flavor. Newsreel footage of the Willard-Dempsey fight is skillfully edited into the story (originally tinted in sepia for theatre release) but it was tipping the scales of credibility just a bit, for the first fight broadcast was actually some years later than the 1919 story would have it. *Variety*, commenting on the fight footage, said, "Insertion of the clips is one of the best examples of expert production judgment and editing of the past year."

In truth BROADCAST was another in a series of photoplays in which Alice was made to suffer before the final reel's romantic windup. Again 20th Century-Fox missed the boat in failing to provide authentic 1920's costumes. Alice's gowns were all 1941 modern and the observing patron would not fail to notice a chorus line wearing the same costumes used three years before in ALEXANDER'S RAGTIME BAND.

Thomas M. Pryor writing in the *New York Times* said, "This latest 20th Century-Fox song-fest is easily the best musical to come this way since that same studio's ALEXANDER'S RAG-TIME BAND of a few seasons back. A streamlined job of songplugging, comedy, and specialty turns, THE GREAT AMERICAN BROADCAST races from one number to the next like a limited making up time. And that is how musicals should be made."

Photoplay for July claimed that, "This is a mighty entertaining picture with its catchy songs put over as only Alice can put them over and its broad humor slapped on as only Oakie can slap it." England's *Daily Film Renter* proclaimed it

With Jack Oakie.

With John Payne.

was a film "put over with verve and vivacity by an accomplished stellar team. Alice Faye sings like a dream."

An additional song entitled "Run Little Raindrop, Run" was written for THE GREAT AMERICAN BROADCAST, and sheet music was published saying "Sung by Alice Faye." Whether Alice ever recorded the song or filmed it is not known, but the Gordon-Warren song appeared the following year in SPRINGTIME IN THE ROCKIES — sung by Betty Grable and John Payne. This film was written for Alice, but motherhood prevented her starring in it.

Weekend in Havana

A 20th Century-Fox Picture 1941

With Carmen Miranda and Cesar Romero.

CAST:

Nan Spencer	ALICE FAYE
Rosita Rivas	CARMEN MIRANDA
Jay Williams	JOHN PAYNE
Monte Blanca	Cesar Romero
Terry McCracken	Cobina Wright, Jr.
Walter McCracken	George Barbier
Boris	Sheldon Leonard
Rafael	Leonid Kinskey
Arbolado	Billy Gilbert
Driver	Chris-Pin Martin
Mr. Marks	Hal K. Dawson
Captain Moss	William Davidson
Tailor	Maurice Cass
Passengers	Leona Roberts
	Harry Hayden

CREDITS:

Director	Walter Lang
Producer	William Le Baron
Original Screen play	Karl Tunberg
	Darrell Ware
Dances Staged by	Hermes Pan
Director of photography	Ernest Palmer A.S.C.
Technicolor director	Natalie Kalmus
Associate	Morgan Padelford
Musical direction	Alfred Newman
Art direction	Richard Day
	Joseph C. Wright
Set direction	Thomas Little
Film Editor	Allen McNeil
Costumes	Gwen Wakeling
Makeup	Guy Pearce
Sound	E. Clayton Ward
	Roger Heman

SONGS: "Tropical Magic," "A Weekend in Havana," "The Nango (Nyango)," "When I Love I Love," "The Man with the Lollipop Song" by Mack Gordon and Harry Warren. "Romance and Rhumba" by Mack Gordon and Jimmy Monaco.

Released October 17, 1941. Running time 80 minutes.

SYNOPSIS: When her cruise ship to Havana runs aground off the coast of Florida Nan Spencer, a hosiery salesgirl from Macy's, refuses to sign a company waiver saying the steamship company was not responsible for the accident. Acting under orders from McCracken,

Jay flies her on to Havana, puts her up at the best hotel, and sets out to show her a good time while back in New York his fiancee Terry must postpone their wedding.

Nan's idea of a hot time is not a visit to Cuba's sugar cane fields with Jay. She suggests the Casino Madrilena, recommended by the bellhop Rafael, where the headline attraction is bombastic Rosita Rivas. At the casino that evening Nan is dismayed at Jay's lack of romantic drive in such an exotic setting. They part company; Nan goes off on her own and meets Monte, Rosita's compulsive gambler-manager, who mistakes Nan for a wealthy tourist.

Next day in the gambling casino Monte convinces Boris, the manager, to credit his overdue account with a percentage of Nan's losses. However, Nan wins, and Monte is deeper than ever in debt until Jay agrees to make up the losses as long as Monte keeps Nan happy.

Complications arise when Rosita decides that Nan is on the make for Monte. Jay escorts Rosita to a little inn in the country and offers to be her new manager until the jealous entertainer spies Monte escorting Nan to the same inn for a midnight supper. Rosita is furious, Monte sheepish, Jay contrite, and Nan dismayed at the deception. She starts back to town alone followed by Jay who only succeeds in wrecking his car.

With John Payne and Cesar Romero (dancing to "The Nango".)

With Cesar Romero and Carmen Miranda.

Alone on the road the tropical magic of the night is too much for them and they fall into each other's arms.

Next morning while they breakfast in his suite Terry arrives with fire in her eye. Nan is broken-hearted and later signs the waiver for Terry who gives her a check for $1,000. Nan in turn gives the check to Monte to clear up his gambling losses. By a stroke of fate Monte wins a fortune at the casino. Nan retrieves the check and sends it to Jay as he and Terry depart by clipper for N.Y. Jay, dismayed at Terry's tactics, leaves the plane in Miami and returns to Nan in Havana. Monte, broke again, begs Jay's help, but with eyes only for her, Jay joins Nan for a fast-paced finale of rhumba rhythms.

NOTES AND REVIEWS: ''WEEK-END IN HAVANA is frothy, gay and tuneful, a pleasant treat for the eyes and ears,'' exclaimed *Photoplay*'s December issue. It was in truth one of the brightest of all Faye films, lushly filmed in Technicolor and edited to a breezy eighty minutes with all the finesse which set Fox musicals head and shoulders above their competitors during this period.

At the helm was director Walter Lang who had made TIN PAN ALLEY the previous year

With John Payne.

On the terrace set—filming "Tropical Magic" number.

On the country road set with director Walter Lang and John Payne.

154

such a success. Lang had a particular feel for musicals and some of the best of the decade were made under his competent direction. Faye was costarred with John Payne for the third time in less than two years, and audiences began to view them as a romantic duo with even more favor than the Power-Faye combination of '38-'39. Special praise was due Ernest Palmer in charge of photography. His sweeping montage sequences admirably and lovingly zeroed in on Havana's most scenic spots providing a tropical locale obviously missing in Faye's THAT NIGHT IN RIO a few months before.

Alice, now the wife of band leader Phil Harris, announced during filming of HAVANA that she was expecting a child the following May. Dorothy Manners writing in the *Los Angeles Times* declared, "Falling in love has had a noticeable effect on Alice Faye. She's never looked so beautiful nor manifested so much verve as she does in this movie. Alice's sad eyes have acquired a new sparkle very becoming in the Technicolor close-ups and the touch of devilishness is most attractive. And what clothes the gal wears!"

Originally slated for three vocal spots, Alice ended up with two — "Romance and Rhumba" and "Tropical Magic," the latter one of her finest screen numbers. A third number, "The Man with the Lollipop Song," recorded and

With Cesar Romero and Billy Gilbert.

filmed, was dropped from the release print and heard only briefly as Payne approached the door of the country inn run by Billy Gilbert.

According to the original shooting script WEEK-END IN HAVANA was to be titled HONEYMOON IN HAVANA. Betty Grable was also slated at one point for the role of Nan Spencer.

Carmen Miranda had one of her best roles in HAVANA, and though her career was relatively brief (this was number three of fourteen screen appearances) she made a vivid impression and was vastly popular with audiences. Ironically Chris-Pin Martin was given prominent billing ahead of Billy Gilbert. His footage in the release print consisted of a thirty-second bit as a driver of a sugar cane wagon with not a word of dialogue.

Hermes Pan's finale production number headed by Miranda was a standout with its flashing colors and intricate footwork on a glistening black floor. John Hobart, writing for a San Francisco review, lauded, "La Miranda has pep, and when she's around 'WEEK-END IN HAVANA' fairly sizzles." In the film's final moments the censors completely overlooked a dancing extra who brazenly fondled the breast of a startled chorus girl. Her look of indignation as she pushed his hand down was a hot item for the rigid code at the time.

But HAVANA was purely Faye's picture all the way. *The Los Angeles Herald Examiner* proclaimed, "Alice Faye looking more sumptuous than ever with her blonde hairdo — Technicolor and a breath-catching wardrobe gives appealing naturalness to the character of the N.Y. girl snatching at romance."

With John Payne.

With Leonid Kinskey (a "killed" still—never used or published.)

On the hotel suite set with director Walter Lang and Leonid Kinskey.

Hello, Frisco, Hello

A 20th Century-Fox Picture 1943

CAST:

Trudy Evans . . . . ALICE FAYE
Johnnie Cornell . . . . JOHN PAYNE
Dan Daley . . . . JACK OAKIE
Bernice . . . . LYNN BARI
Sam Weaver . . . . Laird Cregar
Beulah . . . . June Havoc
Sharkey . . . . Ward Bond
Cochren . . . . Aubrey Mather
Ned . . . . John Archer
Colonel Weatherby . . . . George Barbier
Aunt Harriet . . . . Esther Dale
Missionary . . . . Frank Darien
Burkham . . . . Harry Hayden
Cockney Maid . . . . Mary Field
Opera Singers . . . . Fortunio Bonanova
Gino Corrado
Adia Kuznetzoff
Roller Skating Specialty . . . . James Sills
Marie Brown
Child Dancers . . . . Jackie Averill
Jimmie Clemens, Jr.

CREDITS:

Directer . . . . Bruce Humberstone
Producer . . . . Milton Sperling
Screenplay . . . . Robert Ellis
Helen Logan
Richard Macauley
Musical sequences
Dances staged by . . . . Val Raset
Costumes . . . . Helen Rose
Supervised by . . . . Fanchon
Directors of photogrpahy . . . . . . Charles Clarke, A.S.C.
Allen Davey, A.S.C.
Technicolor consultant . . . . Natalie Kalmus
Associate . . . . Henri Jaffa
Art direction . . . . James Basevi
Boris Leven
Set decorations . . . . Thomas Little
Paul S. Fox
Film editor . . . . Barbara McLean
Makeup artist . . . . Guy Pearce
Special photographic effects . . . . Fred Sersen
Sound . . . . Joseph E. Aiken
Roger Heman
Musical direction . . . . Charles Henderson
Emil Newman

Released March 26, 1943. Running time 98 minutes.

SONGS: (New) "You'll Never Know" by Mack Gordon and Harry Warren.

Singing 'Why Do They Always Pick on Me?"

(Old) "Ragtime Cowboy Joe" by Grant Clarke, Maurice Abrahams and Lewis F. Muir. "San Francisco" Bronislaw Kaper, Walter Jurmann and Gus Kahn, "Lindy" Irving Berlin, "Hello, Frisco, Hello" Louis A. Hirsch and Gene Buck, "Sweet Cider Time" Percy Wenrich and Joseph McCarthy, "Grizzly Bear" George Botsford and Irving Berlin, "Why Do They Always Pick on Me?" Harry von Tilzer and Stanley Murphy, "Bedelia" Jean Schwartz and William Jerome, "Has Anybody Here Seen Kelly?" Charles Moore, C. W. Murphy and William J. McKenna, "Silvery Moon" Gus Edwards and Ed Madden, "Gee, But It's Great to Meet a Friend from Your Home Town" James McGavish, Fred Fisher and William G. Tracey, "He's Got a Gal in Every Port" (composer unknown). "It's Tulip Time in Holland" by Richard A. Whiting and Dave Radford.

With Lynn Bari, John Payne, June Havoc, Jack Oakie and Esther Dale.

SYNOPSIS: San Francisco's Barbary Coast is the hub of light and gaiety for a bustling young metropolis, while at Sharkey's Colosseum Trudy, Johnnie, Dan, and Beulah offer divertissement. Trying out a new number, the group pulls the paying customers away from the bar, and they are promptly fired for their efforts. Trudy begs Dan and Beulah to stick with Johnnie who is full of ideas. When fast-talking Sam Weaver happens upon Johnnie with another tale of a sure gold strike Johnnie grubstakes him to his final $10. Coming upon a missionary group, Johnnie makes a proposition which will benefit them all. He stages a series of street carnivals in front of the saloons which attract the crowds to the ruination of the gin-mills. Each proprietor offers $500. if Johnnie will keep away from his place, but to Sharkey the price is $1,000. With the money from his high-handed blackmail Johnnie opens The Grizzly Bear and becomes an overnight sensation with Trudy as the star of an elaborately mounted show which even brings in the carriage trade from Nob Hill including the haughty Bernice Croft and her entourage. When Johnnie meets this aristocratic heiress he is fascinated by her poise and social position.

The Grizzly prospers and shortly Johnnie opens three more places which makes him an impresario and Trudy the toast of the Coast. One night an admirer named Ned brings Cochran, an English theatrical producer, to see the show, and the enthralled gentleman offers Trudy a starring role in his next London production. Trudy, now deeply in love with Johnnie, refuses, but Johnnie, eager for society prestige abruptly marries Bernice so that he can climb Nob Hill. Broken-hearted Trudy sails for England where as the star of "The Girl from Piccadilly" she is the darling of the London theatre crowds.

Back in San Francisco after a European honeymoon during which time he managed to see Trudy's show, Johnnie's fortunes decline when he tries to sponsor grand opera, long a pet project of his wife. One by one he closes his Coast establishments including even the Grizzly as his wife's demands drain away his resources. Dan and Beulah go back to Sharkey's and Johnnie is a barker for a cooch show on the midway. Trudy returns to sadly find the familiar night spots shuttered and silent. She quietly finances Sam, who in turn convinces Johnnie that he has

The "Silvery Moon" number.

at last struck a gold bonanza. With "his share" of the old grubstake Johnnie reopens the Grizzly but refuses to hire Trudy for his show. The opening is a huge success, the old crowds return, and at the end of a gala number starring Dan and Beulah, Trudy is brought onstage where she is reunited with Johnnie to the strains of "Hello, Frisco, Hello," the number they introduced long ago.

NOTES AND REVIEWS: Returning to the screen after an absence of over a year, Alice Faye was warmly greeted in a vehicle seemingly tailor-made for her special talents as the leading female vocalist of her studio. Dressed in beautiful period costumes she was more lovely than ever before with a tiny waist never seen in her previous pictures.

Her voice seemed to have acquired a fresh, warm maturity ideally suited to introduce "You'll Never Know," the song which became as distinctively Alice Faye's as "Mammy" had been for Jolson. It was a surprise to no one when the number took the 1943 Oscar as Best Original Song, for its wistful lyrics perfectly expressed the war-weary frustrations of women waiting for the return of their men.

In all, Alice sang ten songs, a record for any of her films. but once again one number, "I Gotta Have You" was cut before the film went into release. Many reference books still erroneously list this number as one of three original songs written for the film. Wartime cutbacks and limitations seemed not to affect the production in any way unless the critical person spotted the middle-aged chorus boys in "Doin' the Grizzly Bear" number. Sets were opulent, costumes

161

With John Payne and Jack Oakie.

stunningly vivid in their Technicolored hues, and there was music everywhere. Little wonder that the film is one of Alice's two favorite screen appearances (the other was ALEXANDER'S RAGTIME BAND).

For the opening in San Francisco attended by Hollywood personalities led by Lynn Bari, a mildly irate citizenry, perhaps aided by studio publicists, added extra sparkle to a happy box-office by a slight alteration of the title to HELLO, SAN FRANCISCO, HELLO, the "Frisco" abbreviation always having been a sore spot with the Golden Gate metropolis.

The critics made much of Alice's return which was touted in some circles as a comeback. "Alice Faye returns to the screen in a role that shows her to superb advantage. If it was the aim of Fox to celebrate her return to the screen with a blaze of glory the studio's purpose is stunningly achieved," said *Film Daily*.

"The return of Alice Faye to motion pictures after a charmingly domestic recess is being celebrated with due and touching sentiment by Twentieth Century-Fox in a film which has all the standard qualities of a plush souvenir. It should afford a most pleasant reunion between Miss Faye and her loyal fans." Bosley Crowther in *The New York Times*.

"The most cheerful cinema event of the day is Alice Faye's return in a gay tuneful musical. The singing star is more beautiful and happier looking and has lost none of her ability to put over a song effectively." *New York Daily News*.

"Alice's singing of 'You'll Never Know' and the duet between John and Alice of the title song is one of those moments of movie history not to be forgotten. There is something wistfully plaintive in la Faye's voice that tugs away at the love strings of a body's heart. In her belaced, beplumed, and befurbelowed gowns of the Gay Nineties, Alice is a picture of loveliness." *Photoplay*.

"Alice Faye, after an interval out for maternity, returns to the screen to do her best singing in the showy, kaleidoscopic musical, 'Hello, Frisco, Hello.' Her singing is quieter, more composed, very effective. The Technicolor cameras deal handsomely with her also, presenting her most attractively in the flashy raiment of the Barbary Coast entertainer of the period, amidst gorgeous if bizarre background of the prevailing honkytonks and the contrasts of Nob Hill." *Variety*.

162

With John Payne.

The Gang's All Here

A 20th Century-Fox Picture 1943

CAST:

Eadie Allen .... ALICE FAYE
Dorita .... CARMEN MIRANDA
Phil Baker .... HIMSELF
Benny Goodman and his orchestra .... THEMSELVES
Mr. Mason, Sr. .... Eugene Pallette
Mrs. Peyton Potter .... Charlotte Greenwood
Peyton Potter .... Edward Everett Horton
Tony DeMarco .... Himself
Andy Mason .... James Ellison
Vivian .... Sheila Ryan
Sergeant Casey .... Dave Willock
Maybelle (Hat check girl) .... June Haver
Girl by the pool .... Jeanne Crain
Maid .... Lillian Yarbo
Doorman .... Frank Darien
Specialty dancer .... Miriam Lavelle
Jitterbug dancers .... Charles Saggau
                                   Deidre Gale
Marine .... Frank Faylen
Sailor .... Russell Hoyt

CREDITS:

Direction .... Busby Berkeley
Producer .... William Le Baron
Screen play .... Walter Bullock
   Based on a story by .... Nancy Winter
                                   George Root Jr.
                                   Tom Bridges
Director of photography ... Edward Cronjager, A.S.C.
Technicolor director .... Natalie Kalmus
Musical directors .... Alfred Newman
                                   Charles Henderson
Art directors .... James Basevi
                                   Joseph C. Wright
Set decorations .... Thomas Little
   Associate .... Paul S. Fox
Film editor .... Ray Curtiss
Costumes .... Yvonne Wood
Makeup artist .... Guy Pearce
Special photographic effects .... Fred Sersen
Sound .... George Leverett
                                   Roger Heman
Dances conceived & directed by ...... Busby Berkeley

Released December 24, 1943. Running time 103 minutes.

SONGS: "No Love No Nothing," "A Journey to a Star," "The Lady in the Tutti-Frutti Hat," "The Polka-Dot Polka," "You Discover You're in New York," "Paducah," "Minnie's in the Money" by Leo Robin and Harry Warren. "Brazil" by Ary Barroso and S. K. Russell.

Publicity still with Phil Baker and Carmen Miranda.

SYNOPSIS: Eadie Allen is a member of the chorus at the Club New Yorker where the main attraction is Dorita, colorful Brazilian bombshell. Sergeant Andy Mason stops in to talk with Phil Baker and encounters his father nightclubbing with his neighbor, the nervous, ill-at-ease Peyton Potter. Andy spies Eadie and follows her to a nearby canteen where she helps out between shows. They dance and Andy is beginning to fall in love. Later at the club Eadie arranges for Andy, whom she knows only as Casey, to see the show from backstage. After the show she joins him on the Staten Island ferry where she gives him a preview of a number

*With Carmen Miranda
and Sheila Ryan.*

which is to be her starring spot in the club's next show.

The following day Eadie says goodbye to Andy who leaves for duty in the Pacific and they start corresponding. Months pass, the war rages in the Pacific, and Eadie is now starring at the club, singing nightly to a picture of Andy. When Mason learns that Andy, now a hero, is coming home on leave he arranges to stage the New Yorker's show in Potter's rose garden, the proceeds going to buy war bonds. Members of the show are housed in the Mason and Potter homes where Mrs. Potter recognizes Baker, an old friend from her Paris past when she was a free spirit.

Dorita stumbles upon a disturbing coincidence — not only is Eadie in love with Andy but Vivian Potter is unofficially engaged to him as well. When Andy arrives, Eadie tells Vivian she is in love with Casey, Andy's buddy. Hurt and confused, Eadie continues in the show with Vivian rushed in as replacement for Tony De-Marco's dancing partner. The show goes on amid the lush surroundings of the Potter estate with colored fountains, Benny Goodman's music, and an enthusiastic audience applauding Eadie and Dorita.

Just before the finale Eadie overhears Vivian tell Tony she'll become a permanent member of the show. Eager to find Andy, Eadie is rushed on stage by Mr. Mason who promises to relay the news to Andy. The show's conclusion finds Eadie and Andy with their heads together.

NOTES AND REVIEWS: Upon the completion of THE GANG'S ALL HERE Alice Faye's musical career was nearly ended. She would sing on screen just once more before a voluntary retirement which would last nearly two decades. The film was a financial blockbuster; its theme of wartime romance, lavish color photography, and comedy hijinks ideally suited to the war years. As might be expected, it is dated by today's standards, is never revived in theatres nor shown on television. Essentially it is not good Faye. Pregnant with her second child through much of the shooting schedule, she did not feel well, and at times seemed almost bored.

It is the only time that Alice was directed by Busby Berkeley, who in essence hardly directed at all, allowing his cast to walk through a routine story. But the musical production numbers were quite another matter for the master showman. Miranda's "The Lady in the Tutti-Frutti Hat" was a noisy cornucopia of sounds and breathtaking color with its luscious leggy chorines, tropical settings, and outrageous patterns woven by the girls wielding some gigantic phallic-like bananas and oversized strawberries which defied description. Theodore Strauss writing in *The New York Times* agreed. "THE GANG'S ALL HERE is a series of lengthy and lavish production numbers all arranged by Busby Berkeley as if money was no object but titillation was. Mr. Berkeley has some sly notions under his busby. One or two of his dance spectacles seem to stem straight from Freud and if interpreted, might bring a rosy blush to several cheeks in the Hays office." The spectacular finale left audiences agog with masses of neon lights, more girls (wearing absurdly wrinkled tights) rolling discs of brilliant hues, and a kaleidoscope with Faye as the focal point. Colors assaulted the eye in most delightful fashion to the strains of "The Polka Dot Polka," but the final chorus with principal cast members warbling "A Journey to a Star" with only their heads poked through a curtain failed to come off.

Of the eight Leo Robin-Harry Warren songs heard, Faye stood out in three: "No Love No Nothing" and "A Journey to a Star" were perfectly suited to her quiet, emotional delivery. The "Polka" number was more imaginatively staged with dancing youngsters in period costumes providing support. Three songs: "Pickin' on Your Mama," "Sleepy Moon," and "Drums and Dreams" were cut from the production before release.

In the supporting cast Miranda again had a field day, and her scenes with Horton, whom she playfully called "Potty," were riotous. Charlotte Greenwood's long legs figured hilariously into the garden party sequence as she danced with a teenager whom she quickly outclassed. Ellison, one of the few leading men under forty and ambulatory in wartime Hollywood, was out of place in the sophisticated settings, his forte being innocent family comedies or westerns. Two attractive young starlets began their screen careers in THE GANG'S ALL HERE. Much would later be heard of June Haver and Jeanne Crain. The former was seen very briefly in the opening sequences as a hat check girl who relieves Horton of his chapeau. Crain, dressed in a bathing suit, was spotted much more prominently beside the Potter swimming pool and had one line of dialogue. "Aren't you going in, Mrs. Potter?" she asked Charlotte Greenwood. "Mercy no," replied Greenwood savoring one of the film's best lines. "The pool is Vivian's department. I just have the towel concession."

Critics felt the film was a dressy bit of showmanship as evidenced by *Variety* who chirped, "Alice Faye, sumptuously gowned by Guy Pearce,* sells the two top tunes full value and gives the showgirl role benefit of her personality to click."

Photoplay thought it a confection more aptly named, " 'You've Never Been So Beautiful Before,' " could well be the theme song of this overlavish, plush-cushioned production, so beautiful to look at, so lovely to listen to, but so fragile in story it floats like a feather. However, you're sure to enjoy the picture — it's done-up-brown entertainment."

*This was a minor error. Pearce handled makeup, and the gowns were the work of Yvonne Wood.

With Dave Willock, James Ellison and Sheila Ryan.

With James Ellison.

Four Jills in a Jeep

A 20th Century-Fox Picture 1944

With George Jessel.

CAST:

As Themselves .... KAY FRANCIS
CAROLE LANDIS
MARTHA RAYE
MITZI MAYFAIR

with
JIMMY DORSEY and his Orchestra

JOHN HARVEY   PHIL SILVERS
and introducing
DICK HAYMES as Lt. Dick Ryan
and the guest stars

ALICE FAYE   BETTY GRABLE
CARMEN MIRANDA
GEORGE JESSEL Master of Ceremonies

CREDITS:

Director .... William A. Seiter
Producer .... Irving Starr
Screen play by .... Robert Ellis
Helen Logan
Snag Werris
Story by .... Froma Sand
Fred Niblo Jr.
Based on the actual experiences of Kay Francis, Carole Landis, Martha Raye and Mitzi Mayfair
Music and lyrics .... Jimmy McHugh
Harold Adamson
Musical numbers staged by .... Don Loper
Musical direction .... Emil Newman
Charles Henderson
Director of photography ..... Peverell Marley, A.S.C.
Art directors .... James Basevi
Albert Hogsett
Set decorations .... Thomas Little
Associate .... Al Orenbach
Film editor .... Ray Curtiss
Costumes .... Yvonne Wood
Makeup artist .... Guy Pearce
Special photographic effects .... Fred Sersen
Sound .... Jesse T. Bastian
Murray Spivack

Released March 17, 1944. Running time 89 minutes.

SONGS: "Crazy Me," "You Send Me," "How Blue the Night," "How Many Times Do I Have to Tell you?" by Harold Adamson and Jimmy McHugh. "You'll Never Know," "I'Yi, Yi, Yi, Yi (I Like You Very Much)" by Mack Gordon and Harry Warren. "Cuddle Up a Little Closer" by Carl Hoschna and Otto Harbach. "(If You Can't Sing It) You'll Have to Swing It" (frequently known as "Mr. Paganini") by Sam Coslow. "No Love, No Nothing" by Leo Robin and Harry Warren. "Over There" by George M. Cohan. "Caissons Go Rolling Along" by Brig. General Edmund L. Gruber.

SYNOPSIS: Kay Francis, wishing to bring entertainment to the boys overseas is encouraged to form a showbiz unit made up of herself, Martha Raye, Carole Landis and Mitzi Mayfair. Before the girls can say snafu they are entertaining troops in such diverse locales as an elegant London mansion, damp English Quonset huts, and in the arid ruins of a North African outpost. Interwoven along the way are guest appearances by radio of such stars as Alice Faye, Betty Grable, Carmen Miranda, and George Jessel. The girls themselves encounter romance enroute, and one, Carole Landis, even marries Ted (John Harvey) in England.

Phil Silvers, Mitzi Mayfair, Martha Raye, Kay Francis and Carole Landis.

NOTES AND REVIEWS: Critical reaction to 4 JILLS IN A JEEP was tepid at best. Bosley Crowther summed it up succinctly in his *New York Times* review when he said, in part, "Also, by virtue of the radio, Carmen Miranda, Betty Grable and Alice Faye are pulled in to warble hit numbers from recent Twentieth Century-Fox films. As a matter of fact, the whole picture has an exploitation tone. The question is whether the public will be impressed in the manner desired."

Variety honestly admitted that "...while pleasing and diverting, plus having good pace, picture is far from socko and may not be relied upon to do outstanding business. However, the exploitation boys have plenty to work with, since the 'Four Jills' of the title afford opportunities. Also, there are plenty of names as an aid."

Photoplay clearly saw the strengths of the film. "Guest stars were Alice Faye, Betty Grable, George Jessel, and Carmen Miranda, which isn't bad guesting."

JILLS is a curious film and not a Faye film by any means, but there was no doubt that her name, a potent screen draw, helped pull in the crowds. And crowds there were. That the film made money and turned a tidy profit wasn't surprising. It was wartime and almost anything made money that reached the screen, for audiences were eager for light-hearted entertainment. JILLS is dated corn today, not aged-in-wood schnapps.

If the film had trouble making up its mind as to what breed of cat it really was the eight songs undoubtedly classed it as a musical. At least three numbers were cut before general release, but at least one preview audience viewed a clever, innocuous tune titled "Snafu." Judged "too hot" for the Hays office, it was quickly excised. It exists today and seems strangely tame, but the meaning of the word at the time struck terror to the hearts of rigid movieland. As delivered by Landis, Raye, and Mayfair it was a breezy number in which the trio innocently begged to be told "what snafu really means." Obviously the studio feared that audiences might also ask that question or worse still, know the answer.

Of the starring foursome in this JEEP all were destined to fade quickly from the screen. Mayfair, for all her clever dancing, her "...pert and fresh little personality that registers delightfully on the screen," as one reviewer put it, faded away first. Apparently there was just too little of everything to qualify as a box-office draw. Kay Francis, the glamorous clothes horse of the thirties and a nifty actress in her own right, was nearing the end of a very successful screen career and would appear in only three more nondescript roles in a poverty-row studio before calling it quits. Landis was to be seen in seven more films, mostly B's, before her death by suicide in 1948. Her final film, THE SILK NOOSE, a Monogram quickie, was released two years later. Even Martha Raye, durable comic with a mouth as big as a barn, a bust equal to the Maginot Line, and a powerful set of pipes made only three more films. She alone has remained a name in the entertainment world and is beloved today for the same type of activities seen in 4 JILLS IN A JEEP.

Dick Haymes and Mitzi Mayfair.

Fallen Angel

A 20th Century-Fox Picture 1945

CAST:

June Mills .... ALICE FAYE
Eric Stanton .... DANA ANDREWS
Stella .... LINDA DARNELL
Mark Judd .... Charles Bickford
Clara Mills .... Anne Revere
Dave Atkins .... Bruce Cabot
Professor Madley .... John Carradine
Pop .... Percy Kilbride
Joe Ellis .... Olin Howlin
Johnson .... Hal Taliaferro
with;
Mira McKinney, Jimmy Conlin, Gus Glassmire, Leila McIntyre, Garry Owen, Horace Murphy, Martha Wentworth, Paul Palmer, Paul Burns, Herb Ashley, Stymie Beard, William Haade, Chick Collins, Dorothy Adams, Harry Strang, and Max Wagner.

CREDITS:

Produced and directed by .... Otto Preminger
Screenplay by .... Harry Kleiner
 Based on the novel by .... Marty Holland
Director of photography ..... Joseph LaShelle, A.S.C.
Music .... David Raskin
Musical direction .... Emil Newman
Art direction .... Lyle Wheeler
 Leland Fuller
Set decorations .... Thomas Little
 Associate .... Helen Hansard
Film editor .... Harry Reynolds
Costumes .... Bonnie Cashin
Makeup artist .... Ben Nye
Special photographic effects .... Fred Sersen
Sound .... Bernard Freericks
 Harry M. Leonard

Released October 26, 1945. Running time 98 minutes.

SONG: "Slowly" by David Raskin and Kermit Goell

SYNOPSIS: Broke and with no prospects, Eric Stanton is kicked off the San Francisco-bound bus in the small coastal town of Walton. In a diner run by Pop, Eric is struck by the beauty of Stella, the sultry waitress. Everyone likes Stella including Dave Atkins, her frequent escort, and the brooding Mr. Judd who comes in to drink coffee just to be near her.

Eric, pretending to be an old friend of Madley, a fake clairvoyant, moves into the hotel with Joe, Madley's leg man. But tickets for the coming "spook show" are not selling due to the power of one Clara Mills, a leading citizen. Eric calls on the Mills sisters and succeeds in making an impression on June. The show is a success, but some of Madley's personal revelations alienate the Mills sisters.

When the professor and Ellis move on to San Francisco, Eric stays behind. He cannot get Stella out of his mind. But Stella wants no cheap affair; she has her sights on a home and ring and will settle for nothing less. Angered by Atkins' interest in Stella, Eric devises a plan. He rushes June into a quick marriage hoping to secure her fortune, ditch her, and marry Stella. On his wedding night Eric leaves the house followed by Clara. The next morning the police discover that Stella has been mysteriously murdered.

Mr. Judd, the retired cop from New York, personally conducts the investigation. He first tries to force a confession from Atkins but really focuses his attention on Eric. Fearful of arrest Eric flees to San Francisco with June, but before they can get the money from the bank there, June is taken into custody. Eric does some fast investigating of his own and returns to Walton and Pop's cafe. When Judd tries to take Eric into

With Dana Andrews.

With Charles Bickford.

custody, the tables are turned and Judd, himself enamoured of Stella, admits he killed the waitress. Eric and June return home to start a new life.

NOTES AND REVIEWS: Alice Faye read and rejected over thirty scripts before settling on FALLEN ANGEL which everyone hoped would be another LAURA. Andrews and Preminger combined their skills as on the previous hit of 1944, and Alice herself approached the assignment with high hopes. It would be a switch from the glossy, formula-type musicals of the past. But in the final editing much of her footage was cut, emphasis was largely shifted to Darnell, and Alice's song, "Slowly," was dropped. In speaking of the film Alice honestly admitted that some of her best scenes were not used, sequences leading up to and including the song made her character more believable and less passive than it became in the final release. "I was terribly upset," she confessed. "I felt the film had been ruined, and feeling utterly at a loss I left the studio. I didn't even go to my dressing room to collect my personal belongings." The bitterness lingered, and it was sixteen years before she returned to make another picture.

Critical response was generally favorable. *Variety* began its review by commenting that "FALLEN ANGEL is 98 minutes on the edge of the seat. The melodrama, of the hard-boiled, oh-yeah school, doesn't let down at any point. Fast, high-tension playing of the piece doesn't let a crime film audience get set for criticism and the show should box accordingly."

The New York Times lauded the three stars, laying the blame for Alice's shortcomings on the script. "As the frustrated adventurer, Dana Andrews adds another excellent tight-lipped portrait [to] a growing gallery. Linda Darnell is beautiful and perfectly cast as the sultry and single-minded siren while Miss Faye, whose lines often border on the banal, shoulders her first straight, dramatic burden, gracefully."

The film did well at the box office, but audiences were confused that Faye did not sing. *Photoplay* lamented, "Alice Faye returns to the screen in the dramatic role of the girl Dana marries for expediency, and she makes her thoughtful and appealing. But we could have used a song in there, Alice."

174

With Dana Andrews.

With Anne Revere and Dana Andrews.

Epilogue

When Alice Faye retired from pictures in 1945 after completing FALLEN ANGEL, she still owed her home studio two films. She seemed in no hurry to fulfill the obligation, for her time was occupied partly by radio work.

But roots grow deep, especially with one who has tasted the sweet nectar of success. Alice let it be known that she might consider another film role. When the project was announced she hoped for Don Ameche as her husband and envisioned a Henry King or Walter Lang as director. STATE FAIR was the vehicle, but Ameche, King, and Lang were elsewhere.

If the result wasn't everything she had hoped it might be, STATE FAIR proved she was still a personable, relaxed actress. Her voice was deeper and somewhat huskier than before, but the warmth was still there. The eyes betrayed a mischievous sparkle. It wasn't an old Alice; it was the Alice of old.

State Fair

A 20th Century-Fox Picture 1962

With Pamela Tiffin.

CAST:

Wayne Frake	PAT BOONE
Jerry Dundee	BOBBY DARIN
Margie Frake	PAMELA TIFFIN
Emily	ANN-MARGARET
Abel Frake	TOM EWELL
Melissa Frake	ALICE FAYE
Hipplewaite	Wally Cox
Harry	David Brandon
Doc Cramer	Clem Harvey
Squat Judge	Robert Foulk
Betty Jean	Linda Henrich
Red Hoerter	Edward "Tap" Canutt
Lilya	Margaret Deramee

with:
Albert Harris, George Russell, Edwin McClure, Walter Beilbey, Tom Loughney, Claude Hall, and Sheila Mathews.

CREDITS:

Directed by	Jose Ferrer
Produced by	Charles Brackett
Music supervised and conducted by	Alfred Newman
Associate	Ken Darby
Choreography	Nick Castle
Director of photography	William C. Mellor A.S.C.
Art direction	Jack Martin Smith
	Walter M. Simonds
Set decorations	Walter M. Scott
	Lou Hafley
Costumes designed by	Marjorie Best
Film editor	David Bretherton
Assistant director	Ad Schaumer
Makeup by	Ben Nye
Hair styles by	Helen Turpin C.H.S.
Special photographic effects	L. B. Abbott A.S.C.
	Emil Kosa, Jr.
Sound	Alfred Bruzlin
	Warren B. Delaplain

Color by De Luxe

Orchestrations	George Bassman, Henry Beau, Bennett Carter, Pete King, Gus Levene, Bernard Mayers
Screenplay by	Richard Breen
Adaptation	Oscar Hammerstein II
	Sonya Levien
	Paul Green
From a Novel by	Philip Stong

Released March 9, 1962. Running time 118 minutes.

SONGS: "It Might As Well Be Spring," "Our State Fair," "It's A Grand Night For Singing," "That's For Me," and "Isn't It Kind of Fun" by Richard Rodgers and Oscar Hammerstein II. "More Than Just a Friend," "It's the Little Things in Texas," "Willing and Eager," "Never Say No," and "This Isn't Heaven" by Richard Rodgers.

SYNOPSIS: The Frake family, full of eager expectations, departs for the Texas State Fair under a shadow of doubt. Doc Cramer predicts something bad will happen to someone while they are gone and is willing to wager five dollars on the premise. Wayne wants only to outclass his rival Red Hoerter in the fair's sports-car event. Margie simply yearns for excitement and a touch of romance. Abel covets the top prize for his hog Blueboy, and Melissa hesitantly holds out hope for her mincemeat, which the family has liberally doctored with brandy.

Accommodations are comfortably friendly at the fair, and Margie sets out alone to quickly find her romance in the person of Jerry, a fast-talking announcer. Wayne is smitten with Emily, a flashy song and dance entertainer with a questionable past. As the days pass the various events bring predictable satisfaction: Blueboy, after a dismal start, finds romance and is named Grand Champion; Wayne makes an impressive showing at the race though he and Emily part company; and Melissa's mincemeat not only takes first prize but is the cause for the intoxication of the mousey Hipplewaite.

Back home Wayne decides in favor of his girl friend Betty Jean, who is waiting for him, and Abel wins the five-dollar bet when Margie, on her way to join Jerry, admits the fair was a terrific success.

With Pamela Tiffin, Tom Ewell and Clem Harvey.

NOTES AND REVIEWS: After an absence of almost seventeen years, Alice Faye's return to the screen was eagerly awaited. She faced Cinemascope cameras for the first time in her career and played a mother. "I never had a son," she quipped on the set, "but I have one now." She and Pat Boone got along famously. The smile of old and the good-humored personality were much in evidence, and even the billing (sixth above the title — she never was lower than third during her early years in Hollywood) failed to dampen her spirits. But the long, hot location in Texas proved to be the most gruelling of her career. She had hoped that Don Ameche would play her husband, thereby reuniting one of the screen's most durable combinations. That Faye fared better than some of her costars was obvious, no credit to Ferrer. Alice had been accustomed to careful, exacting direction and found that of the Oscar-winner-actor-turned-director was too casual and relaxed. Also, filming techniques had changed radically.

The critics unanimously agreed about the direction. *Variety* caustically remarked, "Jose Ferrer's direction has a monotonous air about it — love scene to ferris wheel to alternate love scene to merry-go-round and back again." *The New York Times* dismissed the director by saying, "One could credit Jose Ferrer with maintaining a brisk pace in his direction but he does little to relieve the film's lack of surprise. The observer almost knows what will happen in the next scene."

The production did want for the zippy punch of the previous screen outings of the Frakes. In the Will Rogers-Janet Gaynor version in 1932 Louise Dresser was the mother, and in the Jeanne Crain 1945 remake Fay Bainter was the purveyor of mincemeat. *The San Francisco Chronicle* aptly pinpointed the trouble with this remake by stating, "In spite of color, of music, and of comely personalities, what STATE FAIR lacks most of all is good, healthy vigorous aroma of a country fair, with which one senses director Jose Ferrer is totally unfamiliar."

Of the five new songs Richard Rodgers wrote for the production one was written for Faye in particular. In their house trailer at the fair she admonished daughter Pamela Tiffin to "Never

With Pat Boone, Pamela Tiffin, and Tom Ewell.

Say No to a Man," joined in on "Our State Fair," and joined Tom Ewell for "It's the Little Things in Texas I Love."

Of the six stars, Faye and Ewell came off best as *Variety* noted, "None of the four young stars comes off especially well. Pat Boone and Bobby Darin emerge rather bland and unappealing. Pamela Tiffin's range of expression seems rather narrow on this occasion. Of the four, Ann-Margaret makes perhaps the most vivid impression, particularly during her torrid song-dance rendition of "Isn't It Kind of Fun," the film's big production number. Tom Ewell is natural and amusing as the lovable father, Alice Faye poised, sure and attractively maternal as the lovable mother."

There were moments when a bright ray crept into Richard Breen's script. Near the start of the film Pat Boone asked his mother if she thought Harry, the local farmer interested in his sister, Pamela Tiffin, was exciting. Faye, bustling about the kitchen, replied with that old touch of sly good humor, "I certainly do. I think Harry is about as exciting as watching grass grow!" Unfortunately, this bright originality quickly disappeared, and the remainder of the film lacked the bright sparkle of the previous remake.

It is somewhat ironic that the 1945 version was touted as a Faye vehicle. The studio hoped to cast Faye in the role which went to Vivian Blaine, the part played in this last version by Ann-Margaret.

Postscript

In 1944 20th Century-Fox hastily improvised a 70-minute film entitled TAKE IT OR LEAVE IT, showcasing Phil Baker and his popular radio series of the same name. The story involved a young seaman (Edward Ryan) who was trying to raise money so that his expectant wife could have a noted specialist attend her. Ryan selected the category of "Scenes from Motion Picture Hits of the Past." Among the scenes shown and identified was "The Sheik of Araby" with Alice Faye from TIN PAN ALLEY.

After eleven years away from the screen, Alice Faye returned to the limelight—this time in an expensively mounted revival of the stage musical comedy GOOD NEWS. Rehearsals began in New York in October, 1973 and the show opened to sellout audiences at Boston's Colonial Theater on December 17th. John Payne, who starred with Alice in four of her most successful pictures, is her co-star in GOOD NEWS.

Alice Faye and John Payne together again in GOOD NEWS

Appendix·"Oscars"

1935
Dance Direction
KING OF BURLESQUE
Sammy Lee for "Lovely Lady"
and "Too Good to Be True"

1936
Music—Best Song
SING, BABY, SING
Richard A. Whiting and Walter Bullock
for "When Did You Leave Heaven"

1937
Best Picture
IN OLD CHICAGO

Best Supporting Actress*
Alice Brady as Molly O'Leary
IN OLD CHICAGO

Writing—Original Story
IN OLD CHICAGO
Niven Busch

Interior Decoration
YOU'RE A SWEETHEART
Jack Otterson

Sound Recording
IN OLD CHICAGO
E.H. Hansen

Best Score
IN OLD CHICAGO
Louis Silvers

Assistant Director*
IN OLD CHICAGO
Robert Webb
(This award not given after 1937.)

1938
Best Picture
ALEXANDER'S RAGTIME BAND

Writing—Original Story
ALEXANDER'S RAGTIME BAND
Irving Berlin

Interior Decoration
ALEXANDER'S RAGTIME BAND
Bernard Herzbrun and Boris Leven

Music—Best Song
ALEXANDER'S RAGTIME BAND
Irving Berlin for "Now It Can Be Told"

Music—Best Scoring*
ALEXANDER'S RAGTIME BAND
Alfred Newman

Film Editing
ALEXANDER'S RAGTIME BAND
Barbara McLean

1940
Interior Decoration—Black and White
LILLIAN RUSSELL
Richard Day and Joseph C. Wright

Music—Best Scoring*
TIN PAN ALLEY
Alfred Newman

1943
Cinematrography—Color
HELLO, FRISCO, HELLO
Charles G. Clarke and Allen Davey

Interior Decoration—Color
THE GANG'S ALL HERE
James Basevi, Joseph C. Wright
and Thomas Little

Music—Best Song*
HELLO, FRISCO, HELLO
Harry Warren and Mack Gordon
for "You'll Never Know"

*Denotes winner.

Discography

TITLE	LABEL & NUMBER	MATRIX NUMBER
Shame On You	Bluebird/5175	77619
Honeymoon Hotel	Bluebird/5171	77621
* Nasty Man (not issued)		15421
* Here's the Key to My Heart (not issued)		15422
* Yes to You	Melotone/13220	16066
My Future Star	Melotone/13220	16065
Oh, I Didn't Know	Melotone/13346	16922
* According to the Moonlight	Melotone/13346	16921
* Speaking Confidentially (not issued)		L.A. 379
* I've Got My Fingers Crossed	Melotone/6-03-09	BLA 449
I Love to Ride the Horses	Melotone/6-03-09	BLA 450
* I'm Shooting High	Melotone/6-03-08	BLA 451
* Spreadin' Rhythm Around	Melotone/6-03-08	BLA 452
* Goodnight My Love	Brunswick/7821	LA 1202
* I've Got My Love to Keep Me Warm	Brunswick/7821	LA 1242
* This Year's Kisses	Brunswick/7825	LA 1240
* Slumming on Park Avenue	Brunswick/7825	LA 1241
* Never in a Million Years	Brunswick/7860	LA 1304
* It's Swell of You	Brunswick/7860	LA 1305
* There's a Lull in My Life	Brunswick/7876	LA 1306
* Wake Up and Live	Brunswick/7876	LA 1307
The Letter (with Phil Harris)	Victor/20-4124-A	20-4124
State Fair (soundtrack)	Dot/DLP 9011	
Never Say No to a Man		
Our State Fair		
It's the Little Things in Texas		
Alice Faye Sings Her Famous Movie Hits	Reprise/R9 6029	
You Turned the Tables on Me		
This Year's Kisses		
Never in a Million Years		
The Band Played On		
Moonlight Bay		
You'll Never Know		
No Love, No Nothin'		
You Can't Have Everything		
Alexander's Ragtime Band		
Rose of Washington Square		
You're a Sweetheart		
Never Say No to a Man		
Alice Faye in Hollywood (1934-1937)	Columbia/CL 3068	XLP15027-1A

* original recordings issued in this LP

In addition to the sides Alice Faye recorded for well-known labels, the 78 record enthusiasts
know the value to their collections of soundtrack recordings made at 20th Century-Fox
and bearing their unique label with trademark and typewritten song titles. An astonishing number
of these exist today including songs cut from release prints or for some reason never used.
Some collectors can actually number more of these Fox recordings than they can the Faye recordings
under commercial labels.

*NOTE: Original U.S.A. labels listed for the sides cut in the thirties. However, many
of these sides showed up on other labels like Rex, Romeo, Regal Zonophone and others*

The Many Faces of Alice Faye

On the following pages
the many faces of Alice Faye
are to be found ranging from candid shots
to portraits, from on-the-set singing poses
to scenes cut from finished films,
and from studio publicity shots
to a family portrait.
Commencing with her first year
in Hollywood to her most
recent appearance, these pages offer
Alice Faye in some of her best
remembered roles.
She was one of the screen's
loveliest and most photogenic actresses
whose face was ever changing in mood
as well as characterization.

*Clowning with Jack Durant
between takes
NOW I'LL TELL*

June Mills—FALLEN ANGEL

186

Singing
"I'll See You In My Dreams"
(cut from released print)
ROSE OF WASHINGTON SQUARE

Vicki Adams — THE GREAT AMERICAN BROADCAST

Publicity Shot
1936

Attending
Cathay Circle
Theatre premiere of
"Wee Willie Winkie"
with Tony Martin
1937

187

Trudy Evans
HELLO, FRISCO, HELLO

Singing
"Slumming on Park Avenue"
ON THE AVENUE

Costume Publicity Shot
for "Yes To You"
365 NIGHTS IN HOLLYWOOD

With husband Phil Harris,
Alice Jr., and Phyllis
1952

Stella Kirby
ALEXANDER'S RAGTIME BAND

Publicity Shot
1935

189

Publicity Shot
1935

Nan Spencer singing
"Tropical Magic"
WEEK-END IN HAVANA

Sally Day
"The Minuet In Jazz"
SALLY, IRENE, AND MARY

190

Pat O'Day
LITTLE OLD NEW YORK

Betty Bradley—YOU'RE A SWEETHEART

Rose Sargent—ROSE OF WASHINGTON SQUARE

Singing "International Rag"
ALEXANDER'S RAGTIME BAND

Betty Bradley singing the title song—YOU'RE A SWEETHEART

1968 Portrait

Eadie Allen singing "No Love No Nothing"
THE GANG'S ALL HERE

192

Mona Merrick—ON THE AVENUE

Joan Warren—SING, BABY, SING

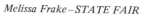
Melissa Frake—STATE FAIR

Peggy Warren in costume for "Foolin' With The Other Woman's Man"
NOW I'LL TELL

Emmy Jordan—BARRICADE